# Communication at Work

### 3rd Edition

## Susan K. Gilmore and Patrick W. Fraleigh

Friendly Press,
2744 Friendly Street
Eugene, Oregon 97405-2255
USA

Paradox Productions, Inc. the parent company for Friendly Press in collaboration with NEM2, Inc. -- New Economy Management Mastery, Incorporated -- presents the 3rd Edition of *Communication at Work.*

The line drawings are the work of James Cloutier.

Friendly Press
2744 Friendly Street
Eugene  OR  97405-2255
USA


Library of Congress Cataloguing-in-Publication Data

Gilmore, Susan K.
Communication at Work, 3rd Edition
Catalog Title No.  80 - 69467


ISBN 0 - 938070 - 09 - 6

We dedicate *Communication at Work, 3rd Edition* to

## George Saslow, M.D., Ph.D.
## and Leona E. Tyler, Ph.D.

Thank you for giving so much for so many years.

Susan and Patrick

# Table of Contents

# Chapter 1

# Introduction to *communication at work*

Whether you are a corporation president, a case worker, a supervisor, a file clerk, a dispatcher, a paramedic, a middle manager, a machine operator, a service provider, a designer, a sales representative, or any other of the forty thousand plus titles in the *Dictionary of Occupational Titles*, you must be able to communicate effectively in order to be successful in your work.  Whether you define *successful* in terms of *personal satisfaction -- what you think and feel about your work --* or in terms of *responsibility and remuneration -- what your workplace thinks and feels about your work --* or in terms of *status and respect -- what others think and feel about you because of your work --*  this fact is clear:

> People who are skillful, constructive communicators are more likely to experience **success** in the workplace.

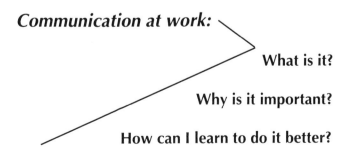

*Communication at work:*

**What is it?**

**Why is it important?**

**How can I learn to do it better?**

> ▲ The Oxford English Dictionary defines
> **communication**
> as the imparting, conveying or exchange of ideas, knowledge etc. whether by speech, writing or sign.

Communication in the workplace involves sending and receiving information. Workers said to be communicating can occupy a variety of space/time relationships to one another. Consider the following connections:

**Letters / memos:** *apart in time; usually apart in space*

**Electronic mail:** *apart in space; usually apart in time*

**Fax:** *apart in space; usually apart in time*

**Telephone:** *apart in space; together in real time*

**Face-to-face encounters:** *together in space and real time*

Communication at work is of the utmost significance; it is a necessary part of planning, executing and evaluating all workplace activities. Everything that happens in the workplace is impacted by the communication -- or *lack of communication* -- about it. Nothing in a workplace goes untouched by the quality of communication within that workplace organization. An organization's purposes for existing can be realized, if -- but only if -- among stakeholders both inside and outside that organization the communication is excellent.

2

Most 21st century organizations will have:

1 declared their values in a mission statement
2 articulated the purposes they pledge guide
  their actions
3 set the goals they are committed to reaching and
4 specified the objectives they will/must accomplish.

However, even the most sophisticated Third Millennium organizations know they are dependent upon the quality of communication -- every day and moment-by-moment -- among their workers. Organizations do not survive, much less thrive, without excellent communication -- valid, reliable and relevant -- among their workers at all levels.

Communication in the workplace could, of course, be improved. Most people will acknowledge that there are, undoubtedly, ways they could improve their skills with the various communication modalities -- letters, memos, FAX's, voice mail, electronic messages, telephone calls, both scheduled appointments and unscheduled face-to-face encounters.

In order to improve your communication at work, you could devote time and energy to acquiring an extensive array of communication **tools** e.g., "I" statements and hypothetical questions. There is no shortage of communication workshops and seminars during which you can be lectured to, demonstrated to and, maybe, be shown a video tape about the latest in communication tools. Typically, such so-called *training experiences* are presided over by highly fluent, sometimes articulate, frequently amusing speakers. Also, you would most likely receive a thick notebook containing more about *how to communicate* than you would ever want to read.

Just imagine for a moment that you were there to learn how to use a set of power tools. Just imagine spending an entire day hearing someone lecturing about using power tools, breaking into small groups to talk about how everyone feels about using power tools, watching someone already skilled with power tools demonstrate some uses for them and then listening again to a list of safety considerations for these power tools. Just imagine that you are allowed to look at the power tools, but you certainly are not allowed to use them in the presence of a person focused on your safety and skills, coaching you and giving you feedback on the skillfulness of your performance or the effectiveness of your efforts to improve.

Most people reading this book would refuse to continue participating in such a charade of training on how to use power tools. Most people reading this book, unfortunately, have sat through equally absurd events which purported to train people on communicating effectively, but which in fact did not involve them in anything approaching *skill practice with coaching.*

The difficulty with focusing on the so-called *tools* of communication is that **training in the skillful use of communication tools** has always been nothing more than making sure people had the latest equipment in their tool boxes -- whether or not they could and did effectively use their tools was not even addressed. As long as you knew the name of the tool and could describe when to use it, your competence with it was never an issue. For example, there have been some ridiculous attempts to evaluate how well seminar attendees could communicate by asking them to write in a workbook what they would say, if they were speaking with someone in a particular situation. Their written words are then read and measured against a list of criteria for effective responses in that situation.

Continuing to use a *tool box metaphor*, everyone's *communication at work tool box* should include a variety of questions -- open-ended questions, multiple choice questions, yes/no questions, probing questions, rhetorical questions, thought provoking questions, etc.

You may have acquired an impressive collection of questioning tools; unfortunately, probably no one has ever coached you on the potential destructive impact of questioning people -- especially poorly executed questioning.

The purpose of this book is to assist you become increasingly skillful communicating at work. This will require your doing more than learning the names of so-called *communication tools.* Your learning to **perform** skills requires significantly more than your learning to recognize and/or understand skillful performance. Learning to understand and appreciate performance -- athletic or musical or dramatic or procedural, for example -- is not the same as learning to perform athletically, musically, dramatically and/or technically.

Everyone agrees that the nature of today's workplace demands that workers are able and willing to use constructive communication skills. But when and where do they learn these specific skills -- when and where do they practice them -- when and where do they prepare to perform them? It is absurd to try to imagine people preparing for job performance in any other skill arena -- music, drama, sports, plumbing, carpentry, design, surgery, laboratory technology, etc. -- just by reading books about it, listening to motivational tapes, having a group discussion or hearing an inspirational speaker explain performance excellence.

As we stated, the purpose of this book is to assist you become increasingly skillful communicating at work. This demands that our recommendations for improving your skills are firmly grounded in a sound theory of how people learn skills. The philosophical foundation and theoretical framework for our work are very important to us. However, we know it is not necessary for others to know or care about the foundation or framework we use in order to benefit from our recommendations.

You do not need to understand automotive intricacies in order to learn to drive an 18-wheeler. But you must know whether you are learning to recognize and appreciate skillful truck driving or you are learning to skillfully drive an 18-wheeler yourself. You do not need to understand how to produce computer software in order to skillfully use a computer. But you would never attempt to develop your computer skills through merely learning the names of software packages.

Communicating at work is an interpersonal process -- not a collection of tools to maneuver people. We view communicating at work with a *personal performance paradigm* focused on skill building. With a *performance* perspective, acquiring *tools* for communicating is much less important than becoming an increasingly skillful *artisan with communication tools.* An appropriate metaphor for this focus would be a young native carver -- honored to be apprenticing to a master carver -- oblivious to the technological crudeness of the carver's primitive tools -- immersed in learning the fundamental skills and techniques used by the master -- **by practicing them.**

When the emphasis is on **performance**, improving your constructive communication skills is accomplished the same way you learn to improve any other set of job performance skills.

---

**People skills should be learned the way other performance skills are learned:**

1  understand what is to be learned
2  have an opportunity to practice where it is safe
3  see and hear your own performance (video feedback)
4  receive constructive feedback from supervisors, peers and subordinates
5  continue to practice and learn in the workplace
6  receive encouragement and corrective evaluation from a coach
7  receive appropriate compensation for skilled job performance

---

The most demanding circumstance for communicating at work effectively is a face-to-face meeting -- scheduled or unscheduled.  Skillfully managing your performance in face-to-face encounters is more difficult because you experience yourself as having less control over what happens.  Even in a situation where there is an agenda, a time frame and you are in charge, the presence of others usually diminishes your sense of control and intensifies your emotional reactions.  Compared to writing a memo about an agenda item, face-to-face discussion/debate is likely to be a more demanding performance situation.

Our focus will be on effective performance in these highly demanding face-to-face encounters.  However, the explanations and skill building suggestions in this book can be applied to all modalities of communication at work.

# Chapter 2

## Assumptions about *communication at work*

"I try not to make any assumptions." "I'm really neutral about a person until I get to know them." "I think I'm pretty objective when it comes to people at work." "I don't like to put people in *categories.*"

You have heard such statements; you may have expressed similar sentiments. On the one hand it is easy to dismiss such statements as **naive.** It is not possible to use language and avoid categorizing and generalizing. It is not possible to observe, think about or conclude anything without categorizing and generalizing. It is not possible to be a sane human without making and acting on some assumptions. It is not possible to be an adult human watching and thinking about other humans and remain neutral -- have no positive or negative thoughts or feelings.

**The encircled statements above are meaningless.**

On the other hand, it is clear that such statements are intended to communicate a view of life that prizes fairness and reasonableness -- that wants to avoid prejudice, bias and bigotry. It is not uncommon for people to choose *meaningless* statements to convey beliefs and values that give their lives meaning. One of the wonderful features of human perception and thinking is that we can process amazingly ambiguous, contradictory, vague, inarticulate, imprecise, nebulous, confused, cryptic, enigmatic, hazy, puzzling, etc. messages from another human and **get it.**

9

The assumptions you pack around about other people will, of course, greatly affect your communication at work with them. The assumptions you pack around about yourself will also greatly affect how you manage yourself regarding communicating at work.

Neutrality or trying to remain *assumptionless* is not possible for humans who communicate with language. Your only hope for being fair and reasonable is to know the assumptive filters you have created and through which information about yourself, people and the world passes.

We have constructed the following set of seven assumptions over the 25 plus years that we have worked together. We pack them along with us as we approach each new teaching/consulting assignment. Additionally, we have observed that people who embrace these assumptions -- when it comes to communication at work -- increase the chances that they will **get it.**

The philosophical underpinnings -- the value footings -- which secure the operating framework within which we teach communication skill building and collaborative problem solving are reflected in the seven basic assumptions which follow.

These seven basic assumptions function as general guiding principles and, of course, are more applicable in some cases than in others.

## It is in your long term best interest to assume:

1 Each person is doing the best that s/he can do at the moment.

2 Each person is unique.

3 Individuals have a great deal in common.

4 Individuals are not out to get you -- it is natural for humans to cooperate, help and share.

5 Constructive communication is demanding and difficult.

6 Improving your communication skills is certainly possible but it probably will not be easy.

7 Interpersonal transactions cannot be reduced to lifeless communication formulations.

This chapter closes with a discussion of these seven basic assumptions.

## 1 Each person is doing the best s/he can at that moment.

In any interaction -- whether with a superior or a subordinate or a peer -- it is in your long term best interest to assume that, regardless of how stupidly, inadequately, ineptly, stubbornly, defensively or self-defeatingly the other person is behaving, that person is doing the best s/he can.   If the person could make a change, either in the way s/he perceived the situation or in the way s/he was taking action in the situation, some improvement might well occur.  But to see things clearly and represent things accurately to oneself and to others, requires a great deal of skill.  It is not a matter of *making up one's mind* and it is done.

Likewise, to take effective action quickly in many situations requires more skill than most people possess -- it is not a matter of *willing it to happen.*  Most instances of so-called carelessness, sloppiness, stupidity, laziness and irresponsibility are not **will problems**, they are **skill problems.**  For example, a person might lack the skills required to critically analyze an ongoing situation:  scanning and focusing, evaluative self-talk and visualization.  Additionally, a person might lack the vocabulary, the fluency, the manual dexterity, the stamina and/or knowledge to carry out a procedure -- particularly under stress.  Finally, a person might lack the self-monitoring skills that are needed for a consistent, steady performance.

The extent to which a lack of skill haunts human interactions in the workplace cannot be overstated!  Because people have been hearing and talking for as long as they can remember, it is difficult for most folks to believe how poorly they listen and how unclearly they explain. They may be able to see how poorly others listen and how poorly others explain. But they usually do not account for interpersonal communication failures as resulting from a lack of skill -- theirs or others. They are more likely to conclude people just aren't trying -- they aren't committed -- rather than conclude people just don't know how -- they aren't competent.

To illustrate, most supervisors would like to do a good job evaluating their subordinates. They particularly would like to view themselves as fair, honest and constructive when delivering negative evaluations. However, few supervisors who have responsibility for the performance appraisal of others would describe the activity as a useful, positive process to which they look forward. Is that because they do not try hard enough or because they are lazy? It is neither one.

Most supervisors are given woefully inadequate job performance appraisal systems and are provided with little -- if any -- training. Few supervisors possess the skills necessary to overcome an inferior evaluation system and create a constructive, collaborative appraisal process.

The reason most supervisors do not do excellent job performance evaluations is that they **do not know how**. They have never been effectively trained to do an excellent job performance evaluation interview. Ask yourself how many supervisors have been coached and allowed to practice the following appraisal skill -- namely delivering negative feedback in a fair and constructive manner.

Very few supervisors, facing the task of delivering negative feedback, possess the skills and knowledge necessary to:

1 Make a clear purpose statement
2 Describe negative aspects of the person's performance
3 State clearly a commitment to assist the supervisee identify behavioral steps to correct deficiencies
4 State the intention to provide support and encouragement for corrective efforts
5 Paraphrase and summarize the supervisee's reactions -- positive and negative
6 Allow time for and encourage discussion

To assume that a person is doing the best s/he can at the moment is not to say that a sub-standard performance must be tolerated. A person's best may be completely unacceptable and if it were not to change, the person may need to be removed or reassigned. But it is in your long term best interest to begin with the assumption that the person is doing the best s/he can and, through your interaction, the performance hopefully will become at least acceptable and, at best, excellent.

Even if the person dealing with you is your superior, you may be able to pull the best from the person by becoming more skillful yourself.

It is in your long term best interest to assume:

**People are doing the best they can.**

## 2 Each person is unique . . . celebrate diversity.

Human beings are so complex and varied it is truly amazing! When we consider the innumerable genetic combinations, the endless variety of child rearing practices, the infinite unplanned life-shaping events that make each of our developmental histories unique, it is no surprise we each perceive, think, feel and act differently.

Of course, it is true that any two humans are more alike than either of them is like a hummingbird or a gopher or even a dolphin. However, the primary feature that sets us apart from all other creatures is an intelligence that allows us to communicate with complex languages, develop technologies, contemplate God, write poetry, plan ahead, enter into contracts and have commitments. This feature also guarantees that we will each be unique.

It is, obviously, quite self-defeating when we fall into the trap of thinking that others are "just like me". We would be well served to go beyond simply resigning ourselves to the differences among us. We need to travel beyond mere *tolerance of our differences.* We need to reach the place where we can respect and celebrate our uniqueness/ diversity. It is the right thing to do!

When you are frustrated with how differently someone sees a situation or you are furious with how someone handled a situation, remind yourself that the diversity among us is inescapable. Aphorisms such as, *it takes all kinds,* and *you wouldn't want everyone to be just the same,* and *variety is the spice of life,* and *one person's meat is another person's poison* -- all help remind us that each person's uniqueness is something to be accepted and savored.

For example, suppose that whenever you must learn a new procedure you learn best by observing a skilled person carrying out the procedure before you are asked to attempt it yourself. Later you may be called on to train and supervise someone who learns best by being given a brief introduction and then a manual to read, followed by an observation session the next day. If you insist upon training the person in the manner that works best for you, you may actually interfere with the person's learning. In most cases, when someone is training a learner in a way that is not good for the learner, it is because the trainer does not know any better. A trainer may not know how to consider differences in preferred learning style or how to adjust training accordingly. The trainer is probably doing the best s/he can and simply does not know how to take into account people's uniqueness.

In the workplace, understanding and accepting each person's uniqueness results in an *appreciation of diversity* characteristic of the most profitable businesses world wide. *Appreciate* means to raise the value of; *appreciate diversity* in the workplace means to seek out, listen to, act on and reward the suggestions of workers from all levels in all areas. Corporations who have appreciated diversity have benefitted greatly from the value-adding suggestions of employees. *Appreciating diversity* appreciates profits. Not only is understanding and accepting diversity the right thing to do -- it is the profitable thing to do.

*Appreciating diversity* does not mean you must mindlessly implement each and every suggestion that employees develop. What it does mean is that people in the workplace are listened to and taken seriously -- especially those workers who are closest to the process or product to which value is being added. Some suggestions are not cost effective, some would be unsafe and some are ridiculous. Judgment must be used by an appropriate panel of evaluators to screen suggestions. *Appreciating diversity* means that productive suggestions are respected and rewarded.

Again, *celebrating diversity* does not mean you must throw away all standards and claim that any one way of doing, seeing, feeling or thinking is as good as another. What it does mean is that you recognize that there is nearly always more than one equally fine way to see, feel, think or act in a particular situation. Some ways of experiencing and/or handling things are, of course, much less preferred -- or even completely unacceptable. But rarely is there just one right way to proceed. Because we are so varied and unique we must accept and encourage differences while maintaining standards.

It is in your long term best interest to assume:

**Each person is unique . . . celebrate diversity**.

### 3 Individuals have a great deal in common . . .
### celebrate unity.

Having carefully established that uniqueness is a special feature of human creatures, it may seem contradictory to now talk about how much alike people are. But, clearly it is not inconsistent to affirm that each person possesses a unique pattern of perceptions, thoughts, feelings and actions, and to acknowledge that people are character- ized by common basic needs and processes.

When humans began reflecting upon their own nature, they undoubtedly observed that people pass through stages in their journey from womb to tomb. While it is true that each person's passage is unique, there are some common landmarks shared by people in the same stage. The purposes and problems with which a person is grappling depend, in part, on the person's life stage.

| LIFE STAGE | PURPOSES/PROBLEMS |
|---|---|
| Infancy | Being cared for -- taking hold of life |
| Childhood | Becoming a proactive person |
| Adolescence | Transition toward independence |
| Young adulthood<br><br>and<br><br>Middle adulthood | Establishing a work; joining with others; responsibility for self responsibility for others; Maintaining a work |
| Late adulthood | Transition toward dependence |
| Old age | Being cared for; letting go of life |

After Erikson, 1959.

## Assumptions about *communication at work*

Deeper understanding of your supervisors at work or the people whom you are supervising, may result from thinking about each person's stage of life. At each developmental stage, people have common concerns regarding dependency, health, personal responsibilities, energy level, resources and opportunities to begin again, fears about the future, etc.

In addition to these age-related common factors, it is possible to identify needs/purposes that **all people** share regardless of their ages:

---

1 Physical safety and well-being.

2 Opportunities to have impact on the environment and on ideas, concepts and systems.

3 Understanding, acceptance and encouragement from others.

4 Possibilities for partially -- at least -- shaping one's own future; choosing where and when to do what with whom.

5 Caring for, sharing, exchanging and cooperating with others.

6 Possibilities for growing, developing, exploring, learning, creating and renewing -- processes which apply to the individual physically, intellectually, emotionally, socially and spiritually.

7 Coming to terms with existential issues: aloneness, ego-centricity, choice, meaning, time and death.

---

To whatever degree you can arrange things in the workplace for yourself and others to feel safe, to have impact, to be understood, accepted and encouraged, to care for, to cooperate, share and exchange with others, to explore, learn and develop personally, and to come to terms with life's basic questions you will be contributing to meeting the basic needs common to us all. The workplace cannot, of course, provide the answer to everything, but it can be designed and operated to contribute significantly to satisfying our common needs and purposes.

It is in your long term best interest to assume:


**People have a great deal in common . . . celebrate unity**.

## 4 Individuals are not out to get you: it is natural for humans to cooperate, help and share.

It is in your long term best interest to assume that individuals are not out to get you. It is true that many systems we have designed are damaging to human beings -- or at least indifferent to people's well-being: e.g., health care delivery to poor people, transportation for older people, architectural barriers for physically handicapped people. It is also true that many people are careless, inept and easily put on the defensive so that it might appear to you that they are out to get you.

It is of course true that sometimes there are individuals in the workplace who are consciously, intentionally, out to get someone. This degree of malevolence is uncommon enough, however, that you do not need to be on guard against it. A specific threat to your life or well-being is a different matter, of course.

If you learn to approach people skillfully, making your purposes clear, listening carefully to their concerns and being open to clarification and/or collaboration, you will find them to be helpful and cooperative nine times out of ten.

The more we learn about the human brain and nervous system, the more evidence we have for understanding that cooperative, helpful, altruistic behavior is not some thin veneer overlaid on a vicious, savage beast whose hostile, aggressive impulses threaten to break through and destroy at any moment. Rather, what is clear is that cooperative, helpful, sharing, altruistic behavior is basic to the human critter and has been part of human programming since early human forms hunted together, sang and danced together, worshipped together, built together and exchanged goods and services. *Community* is as much a natural aspect of being human as migration is for salmon and geese. The mechanisms are different structurally, but the programs are very similar functionally. What is important is that you learn to *trip the switch,* or *push the button* or *call out from the other person -- and from yourself --* the programs designed for cooperative, helpful human transactions rather than *pushing the button* for hostile, uncooperative, defensive programs of interpersonal transactions.

There is a lot in our modern culture that invites people to think only of themselves -- to *get a life,* but to avoid getting overly involved -- to *play it way cool,* but to *want it real hot.* Supposedly, this will result in getting ahead -- or at least not getting behind. Mass media -- television, radio, films, magazine ads, billboards -- carry these self-aggrandizing messages unrelentingly into every corner of our culture. Home, school and church have lost much of their power to transmit believable messages of cooperation and helpfulness. Within a *community* it is difficult to be helpful to one another because everyone is in such a hurry struggling to not lose ground. Family members only occasionally sing, dance and celebrate together. Even families who try hard cannot arrange schedules to regularly eat together. Birth and death occur in isolation. We have lost the benefits of community while acquiring rapid access to information and travel to anywhere -- including the moon.

Nevertheless, it is still true that cooperation and helpfulness are natural for humans and that the most successful humans are cooperative and helpful. People's insensitivity, apparent lack of concern, failure to get involved and seeming unwillingness to lend a helping hand do not result from indifference or willfulness. They are primarily the result of incompetence -- the inability and unfitness to meet and master the demands of a fast moving, socially isolating, mechanized, dehumanizing modern culture. Very few people can single-handedly combat the cultural onslaught.  Horrifying as it is, vast numbers of people these days are grappling with their lives single-handedly -- without the benefit of community.

It is in your long term best interest to assume that it is natural for people to be helpful and cooperative.

It is in your best interest to approach others in a non-threatening manner *calling out the best* by being clear about your own purposes.

It is in your best interest to avoid blaming people for their passive, resistant, inadequate handling of confusing, difficult situations.

It is in your best interest to recognize that few people have adequate support groups, communities, and/or mentors to withstand the mass media message that the *beautiful people* are cool, aloof and self-serving.

It is in your best interest to remember that -- with rare exceptions:
### individuals are not out to get you.


They act that way because they are incompetent and/or scared.

## 5 Constructive communication is demanding and difficult

When people are gathered, two or more in the same general space, it is impossible for them not to communicate. If no one says a word, certainly that communicates a great deal. If only the men speak and the women just listen, that says a lot. Communication -- whether or not it is constructive, neutral or destructive -- is inevitable. Unless you remain isolated from all other people, you cannot decide to *stop communicating*.

Although you cannot avoid communicating, consistently choosing constructive communication is another matter. Constructive communication is difficult and demanding, not because people are basically devious and defensive and destructive, but rather because human thoughts, perceptions and feelings are so complex and language is very ambiguous.

We are often faced with trying to convey what we may not fully understand about an interaction or process which does not and never will exist. Neither our limited understandings nor the interaction in question has *thing properties* -- they do not exist . *Things* exist in time and space; you can take photographs of *things*. It is not too difficult to talk about *things* unambiguously -- where to locate them, how much we should have on-hand, whether we need more, etc. Intelligence, motivation, TQM, CQI, empowerment, trust, leadership, cooperation, collaboration, etc. are not *things*. It is not easy to talk about our perceptions, thoughts and feelings unambiguously. The most important communication at work is not about *things*.

The chart below is an effort to help manage the complexity of human communication. Reference will be made to two dimensions: 1) receiving, processing, sending; 2) verbal and non-verbal.

|  | Verbal | Non-verbal |
|---|---|---|
| Receiving | *Paraphrasing* | Observations of changes in voice, skin and body movement |
| Processing | *Performance Imaging* | Attending, relaxing |
| Sending | *Purpose stating* | Voice quality Facial expression Gestures: face & hand |

We have a strong bias that focusing on non-verbal factors contributes very little to mastering fundamental communication skills. We believe that non-verbal factors are less important than the verbal aspects of interpersonal communication. Clear transmissions and clear reception of interpersonal messages are more dependent upon the use of language than the use of gesture, posture and facial expression.

Learning the fundamental skills of receiving, processing and sending messages is presented in Chapter 5 entitled **MasterSkills® for communication at work**. Despite the complexity and ambiguity, you can decide to begin becoming a very skillful, constructive communicator. By working hard, practicing the correct techniques, receiving accurate, timely feedback about your performance and practicing more, you can expect to meet the demands and overcome the difficulties inherent in human communication.

The *personal performance paradigm* for learning communication skills introduced in Chapter 1 requires that
learners be able to review their own performances in a
safe setting with constructive coaching. Most typically
this will involve viewing a video tape of your own efforts
to communicate effectively. Fortunately, most non-verbal features of your performance will automatically improve without conscious effort on your part as you are
working directly and consciously on the verbal aspects of
your performance.

Instead of worrying about the non-verbal cues you may
unwittingly be sending, spend your energies learning to
send clear, accurate verbal messages. Instead of worrying
about discerning the non-verbal cues other people may
be giving off, learn to listen very skillfully to what they
actually have said to you.

Although we have acknowledged the inherent difficulties
in interpersonal communication -- because people are
complicated and language is imprecise -- we have also
affirmed that it is possible to greatly improve the quality of
communication. The sense of *community* that is possible
among skillful communicators, the appreciation of uniqueness possible among skillful communicators, the mutual
problem solving and cooperation among skillful communicators are each worth the struggle to become more
skillful. **Constructive communication is difficult and
demanding**, but is certainly worth the effort.

## 6 Improving your communication skills is certainly possible, but it probably will not be easy

Changing the way you communicate is difficult. Any systematic change in the way you do something -- particularly something such as communicating which you have done all your life -- is difficult. The types of behavior changes that people are likely to need and want to make, together with specific examples of communication skill changes are illustrated below:

| Behavior change | Communication skill examples |
|---|---|
| Acquire new behavior | • Learn to **purpose state**<br>• Learn to **paraphrase**<br>• Learn to **performance image** |
| Increase frequency and/or intensity of old behavior | • Nod and smile<br>• Verbally acknowledge that other person's comments are heard |
| Increase consistency of old responses across situations | • **Purpose state** clearly to superiors as well as subordinates<br>• **Paraphrase** even when I know I disagree before I state my objections |

Popular psychology has delivered a gross disservice to many people by implying or stating explicitly that insight into one's shortcomings will begin to correct them. Insight into your need to change -- i.e., why you are the way you are, how you got that way, what defensive purposes are served by your being that way, etc. -- is at best interesting information. Most likely, such information results in your criticizing yourself and feeling guilty about your failure to change what you now *understand*. Unless there is an accompanying program to support a behavior change effort, insight often does more harm than good.

Even the recent self-help programs -- some of which are backed by research demonstrating their effectiveness -- tend to gloss over and minimize how very difficult it is to stay with any self-management program. In general, the self-improvement efforts which are most likely to succeed are characterized by:

1. taking small steps
2. **adding** behavior, not **subtracting** it
3. keeping records
4. encouraging others to cheer you on
5. rewarding success specifically and often

For example, suppose you have been told by more than one person on more than one occasion that you have an unfriendly, unresponsive, aloof way of interacting with people -- particularly if you do not approve of something. You have even been accused of being cold and uncaring. Suppose further, that this *unfeeling, uncaring aloofness* is experienced by yourself as *reserve* and *shyness* and *uncertainty*. So while descriptions of *unfriendliness* and *coldness* are nothing with which you can identify, you can see that if you approach the problem as one of learning to behave differently, you will need to gain insight into what people mean when they describe you that way. You will need to understand what exactly you need to learn to do differently. Insight into why you act that way or how you got that way will be the least useful consideration.

The following examples illustrate a self-improvement effort using the five guidelines listed above and are contrasted with common misguided efforts to change:

## Taking small steps

Focus on one situation with one or two people where your purpose is clear and you can plan for the interaction. Paraphrase, nod and smile while interacting with these people twice a day in the beginning.

**vs.**

## Taking too large steps

Listening and being friendly is not such a big deal -- it is, after all, just being polite. Tell yourself you should be able to be warm, open and friendly to all people whether or not you really like or respect them. Just be more pleasant.

## Adding behavior

For one week prior to your next evaluation interview observe yourself in the mirror twice a day. Pretend you are seated in the evaluation session, then see yourself look at the other person, smile and nod. During the next evaluation interview, paraphrase everything which is said to you before you state your thoughts and opinions -- whether you are evaluating or being evaluated. Incorporate smiling and nodding with the paraphrasing.

**vs.**

## Subtracting behavior

Prior to the evaluation interview, when you are not intent on other things, remind yourself not to frown and not to be so withdrawn, not to avoid eye contact, not to wait for others always to begin conversations, not to be so worried about what others think and whether or not they like you. Stop being so egocentric.

## Keeping records

Write down each day the successes you have had that day with the small step increments which had been planned. You need both a brief narrative account -- e.g., a journal -- and a charted numerical index of progress. The journal should serve as a place to note any unforeseen events that might influence the whole self-management effort and contain a record of the rewards (reinforcers) delivered.

**vs.**

## Letting it flow

Stay loose, hang in there and don't sweat it. By taking a laid back, mellow approach, you can avoid trying to *push the river* and just let things flow naturally. If you truly want something to happen, it will happen. There needs to be a stronger connection between your positive self and what blocks you from being more friendly and open.

## Encouraging others to cheer you on

Assume it is up to you to recruit and train your encouragers. You must like and respect your encouragers. Your encouragers need to care about you, approve of your self-improvement efforts and be willing to be honest with you. Approach the people you want to help you with your program. Assume that you must reassure them that being direct with you by giving honest feedback and encouragement is in your best interest. Assume that you will have to *coach* the people on things to avoid -- pushing you too hard, being overly enthusiastic, having too many suggestions -- that mostly what you need is a rally squad who will cheer when you score points.

**vs.**

## Counting only on yourself

Assume that if someone truly cares about you s/he will notice your self-improvement efforts and will naturally say something to you. Assume that people who know you reasonably well know what feedback would be hard for you to handle. Assume that other people have better things to do than mess with your self-improvement program. Assume that strong, healthy people are rugged individualists who only look to themselves for reinforcement, that turning to others is a dependency you don't need. Assume it is more responsible to rely only on yourself.

One way to view personal responsibility for the mature adult involves holding yourself accountable for arranging the environment in such a way that you are reinforced for doing those things you identify as healthy, mature, adult behavior which may -- for whatever reason -- be difficult to begin or sustain. To quibble over the naturalness vs. artificiality and the intrinsic vs. extrinsic properties of rewards is less important than making certain you are moving forward toward an increase in positive behavior and a decrease in negative behavior. It is better to arrange things so you are rewarded for acting decently and responsibly, than to wait around until you truly feel like it and really want to.

## Rewarding success specifically and often

Plan a reward system so that your early efforts receive a great deal of support. *Getting started* is often the most aversive part of self-improvement programs. Later you can *thin out* the diet of reinforcers. You may need to accumulate points which are then exchanged for a reward. For example, you might receive 1 point for every **paraphrase,** *smile and nod combination,* record points on a wrist counter; for each day you score 5 points or more during week 1 of your program, reward yourself with a long-distance telephone call to someone you probably would not be calling otherwise, but who is a real pleasure to talk with. When you reach a skill level where **paraphrasing** regularly is automatic for you, it may have become intrinsically rewarding.

### vs.

## Letting success serve as its own reward

Doing something well should be intrinsically rewarding. It ought to be reward enough that you know you did your best. Success can be defined as *doing your best,* giving it your all. Success doesn't always mean you will reach your goal. So whether you reach your goal or not, if you did your best, you are successful. If you know you were successful, then you won't need any artificial, extrinsic reward for your efforts. Make up your mind to put your whole self into it, recognizing that things of true value are costly. You can't expect to be rewarded for every good thing you do.

It is a fact that many things you need to change are not now and never will be intrinsically rewarding -- especially in the beginning when you have limited skills. **Playing the game with a purpose, a set of rules and rewards for winning is not *fooling yourself* nor *deceiving others*.** It is a sensible way to manage yourself.

Thus, we say it is in your long term best interest to assume: **improving your communication skills is certainly possible, but it probably will not be easy.** Hopefully, you will recognize the good sense of being patient with yourself and utilizing the best self-improvement strategies available.

## 7 Interpersonal transactions cannot be reduced to lifeless communication formulations.

Imagine that you are driving a car at night along a freeway. You have one passenger with you, seated in the front seat beside you. Imagine that you hear a soft snoring sound, glance over and realize that the person has gone to sleep. Even though there may have been a 15 minute period of silence prior to the snoring when you were both awake but preoccupied with your own thoughts, the instant you realize the person is asleep you are now *alone* in a different way.

Imagine two robots programmed to play chess with each other. They could even be programmed to remind one another whose play it is if there is too long a delay. But there is no way now or in the foreseeable future to ever program into a computer the existential event of *recognizing you are alone in a different way* when someone you are with loses consciousness.

We can systematically assist people with self improvement programs to develop increasingly effective communication skills in the workplace. But we must never lose sight of the fact that the communicators are two or more human beings and that there is *something more* to human communicative transactions than formulae and technology. There are existential dimensions which make every act of communication an organic reality. The individuals are alive, someday-to-die, must-make-choices, never-truly-totally-understood human persons.

Most people have seen or experienced directly, the grim reality that every possibility for constructive communication can be destroyed by violence and neglect. If you actively seek to traumatize with the verbal process -- assaulting, battering, cutting, exploding, ripping, subduing, twisting, wrenching with words -- you or anyone else can single handedly destroy the possibility of constructive human transactions. If you fail to nurture with the verbal process and are instead neglectful -- ignoring, denying, distorting, poking, toying, nagging, harassing, picking, ridiculing, deceiving with words -- you may also be guilty of killing the possibility of constructive human encounter.

One robot communicates something hideous, untrue and unfair to another robot without blowing any circuits in either machine. One computer could lose track of, make a false assertion to or fail to communicate its purpose to another computer. But you would not think to label it careless, lying or risking bad faith/loss of good will. These shameful or embarrassing consequences of ineffective communication belong to living beings.

With this final assumption, we are addressing the ethics of misusing communication skills. Obviously, communication skills can be used destructively -- the tools with which to build can become weapons with which to obliterate. Destructive communication at work is wasteful, cruel and dangerous. Constructive communication at work can restore, build and create.

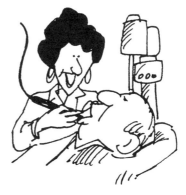

Hopefully, you will agree that people should use their communication skills to:

> 1 increase a positive sense of community -- of belonging and safety and stability.
> 2 increase a positive sense of identity -- of being unique and special and prized.
> 3 increase mutual problem solving, cooperation and sharing.

We invite you to affirm such a position and commit yourself to pursuing it in your workplace. It is in your long term best interest to do so.

# Chapter 3

## Barriers blocking *communication at work*

Most people know that interpersonal communication failures cause serious problems in the workplace. But, unfortunately, they usually believe the problems are there because folks have different **values** or they are just too **emotional** or they aren't really **trying** to communicate. Values conflict, low motivation and emotionality are **not** the biggest barriers blocking communication at work.

Of course values conflict is sometimes at the root of communication difficulty, but that is rarely the problem. Compared to the communication difficulty that stems from people with compatible values becoming deadlocked because neither side has actually listened to the other -- values conflict is a minor problem.

Intense emotion also sometimes keeps people from being able to communicate, however one of the most frustrating events for people in the workplace is communication failure -- communication breakdown is one of the things about which people are likely to become emotionally intense. Emotional intensity is more likely to be a result, rather than a cause of communication failure.

It does not help to try harder to do something for which you do not have the **skills**. Trying harder with insufficient skills only makes a person feel foolish and frustrated. Workplace communication failures are most typically *skill problems -- not will problems.* **The #1 barrier blocking communication in the workplace is lack of skill.**

Nevertheless, there are some general understandings about communication at work that are worth pursuing. We will use a *journey metaphor* to reach those under- standings.

According to the Oxford English Dictionary, *understand- ing* refers to a person having knowledge and judgment - - being discerning, intelligent and sagacious. The OED labels the use of *skill* to mean knowledge or understand- ing as **archaic**. The OED states that *skill*, in contemporary usage, refers to a person having practical knowledge in combination with ability, expertness, as for example in a craft. Clearly the emphasis with *skill* is on a person's ability to do -- to make happen.

Unfortunately, popular writings about human transac- tions in the workplace frequently fail to make this critical distinction between knowing about something and being able to perform something -- such as coaching. Pick up any business/management book or magazine and there you will find hundreds of examples of the archaic use of *skill* to mean special knowledge or understanding -- whether or not the person can **do** anything with the special knowledge.

This failure to distinguish between *skill* and *understanding* is what allows the workplace to send supervisors to a seminar where they are told they should *coach* their people and, since the supervisors know what a coach is and does, expect supervisors will begin doing it. The idea that **understanding** and being **skilled at** coaching are as different as understanding baseball and being able to coach baseball -- somehow gets lost when the skills in question are people skills. People skills can only be seen during interpersonal performance; they require more than interpersonal understanding.

On the other hand, it is not the case that *understanding* has no merit in facilitating effective communication at work. Using our journey metaphor: it takes understanding to plan a journey -- develop an itinerary, chart the waters, file a flight plan -- but driving a van, sailing a ship and flying an airplane require more than understanding. They require *skill* in addition to *understanding.*

This chapter will present and discuss five such *understandings* about interpersonal communication. Chapter 5 is devoted to skill building for communication at work; the present chapter is about the importance of knowing and understanding what blocks communication at work. If you understand the currents, you are less likely to capsize; if the curves are not an upending surprise, you are less likely to crash. Knowing about the weather and understanding instrument flying increases the chances you will not become disoriented when there are no familiar landmarks.

The following five impediments to communication at work will be presented and discussed in order:

- proactive response pattern: unacceptable
- purposes ↔ values: unconnected
- purposes ↔ methods: entangled
- rhythm and timing: inappropriate
- performance expectations: unreasonable

## Proactive response pattern: unacceptable

"Most people travel along doing the best they can, trying to stay out of trouble, reacting to things as they come up. People tend to be **reactive** rather than **proactive**." When we wrote those words in 1985, almost no one reading the material could define *proactive*. Very few people had even heard the word. Now it is a boardroom/breakroom buzzword. Everyone in the workplace knows that individuals, teams, companies, corporations and nations are supposed to be *proactive* -- that's how they will make it in the new global economy.

Unfortunately, *proactive* is typically misunderstood to be merely a new word for *aggressive*. Stop ten people in the workplace, ask them for a definition of *proactive* and you will hear that it means to *get the jump on* or *be a step ahead* in making things happen.

*Proactive* means your performance is *planful, anticipatory and intentional*. The key to developing a *proactive* response pattern is to focus on the correct person -- namely yourself. You need to anticipate the impact *you* would like to have, as well as the impact *you* are likely to have. You need to focus on what *you* are going to do to make things happen. When you are preoccupied with what others are going to do to you or what others should do for you, you are focused on something over which you have no control -- the behavior of other people. You do have the possibility of controlling your own behavior. It is also true that the most effective way to influence others is to become increasingly skillful in managing yourself so that others are more likely to respond to you in ways you regard as favorable.

Developing a proactive response pattern requires viewing future transactions as occasions for your having a planful impact. Anticipating such transactions becomes a process of planning how to handle yourself in order to make your intended purposes more likely to be realized. Developing a proactive response pattern means you anticipate and plan -- you imagine and choose the impact you would like to have. You know you need not merely react as some automated, pre-programmed representative of your family, class, sex, age, race, role, etc. Instead, a proactive response pattern means you can design how you will handle yourself in relation to others. Such a response pattern does not rigidly fix on a view of the future projected primarily in terms of how other people should behave or how you fear they will behave. The focus is on managing yourself.

There are two groups of folks who at least initially may find the position we are presenting unacceptable. There are people -- particularly those with fundamentalist religious backgrounds -- who regard all the emphasis on *self* -- self development, self management, focus on yourself, self talk -- as an unhealthy preoccupation with oneself that cannot help but make a person selfish, ingrown and insensitive to others.

Our position is just the opposite. By acquiring skills for collaborative communication at work, individuals are in the best position to stop worrying about and protecting themselves from imagined enemies. Instead, it is much more likely that proactive, skillful communicators focus on themselves for purposes of accepting responsibility to have a constructive impact and make their transactions mutually beneficial.

The other group of folks who may find our position objectionable are people who are committed to *spontaneity* as a way of life. *Spontaneous* means random -- and that is not really what these folks have in mind. When we talk with these people, usually they are trying to avoid a phony, uptight, contrived life style. They speak of accepting responsibility for their own lives as we do, but *planning* and *self management* -- for them -- have been associated with a rigidly role-bound, mechanistic, non-feeling existence.

Again, our position is just the opposite. Individuals who choose to use communication skills proactively will increase the frequency of open, here-and-now, emerging, growth-producing encounters with others.

Becoming skillful at proactively managing yourself regarding what it is you are trying to make happen and how you intend to make it happen, means you cannot fool yourself about your preferences nor lie to yourself about your motives. Becoming skillful at proactively presenting yourself to others means you will have become skilled in informing others of what you are trying to make happen or would like to see happen or believe should happen. Being proactive with others means you voluntarily tell them about your plans or intentions or view of the future -- they do not have to pry it out of you nor trick you into revealing yourself.

It is true that people who manage themselves proactively and are proactive with others usually are able to make things happen -- because that is where they are focused. They almost never ask, "What's going to happen to me/us?" They direct their attention and energy to "What I/we think should happen and how I/we should proceed."

People who manage themselves proactively are not worried about whether they *should* be so concerned about *shoulds*. It makes sense to them to try to accomplish what will be good and right for themselves and to execute it in the most effective, efficient way they can. Being proactive means being planful and intentional and effective; it certainly does not have to mean being ruthless and self-serving. Making sure that your proactive energies are headed in the right direction and aimed at good and right goals is the focus of our next issue: the connection between values and purposes must be strong and clear.

# Purposes ↔ Values: Unconnected

The second impediment crippling communication at work is the lack of connectedness between the ***purposes*** pursued by people in the workplace and the ***values*** held by those same people.

> For Example: Picture that you are attending a staff meeting with a team leader in charge and trying to move through the agenda. The leader says, "Now's the time to discuss this before we vote -- anybody have anything to say?" You believe some discussion before the vote is very important. You assert what you believe is true by saying, "I think we should hear from everyone on this issue -- I know not everyone agrees." The leader then counters with, "I'm not sure everyone has to speak....there are only so many ways to look at it."

It may seem perfectly obvious to you that your purpose is to ensure there is an opportunity for all people affected by the impending decision/vote to voice their objections, alternatives, concerns, support, etc., knowing that when teams have such an opportunity they are more likely to:

1 find solutions where what appeared to be conflicting purposes get served

2 develop a compromise that does the least damage to the minority

3 provide an opportunity for those on the prevailing side to have respectfully listened to and have heard those who did not prevail.

An opportunity to be respectfully heard increases a sense of fair play, appreciation of diversity and an identity with the team. An opportunity to have been respectfully heard and taken seriously makes it much easier for those team members who must accommodate and support a measure they voted against to act collaboratively.

The statement, "I think we should hear from everyone on this issue -- I know not everyone agrees", comes close to being a clear statement of your purposes rooted in your values, but it falls short. The statement places primary emphasis on **how to** accomplish the purposes (". . .hear from everyone. . .") rather than the value footings.

Examples of clear purpose statements anchored in values are:

> "I know we have big disagreements about this issue and we do a better job afterwards when we make sure everyone feels that people have had a fair chance to be heard -- so I want us to do whatever will guarantee or provide for that."

Or

"I don't care how we do it; I just want us to decide this thing so it has the least chance of tearing up the team -- we need to continue to be a team. . . . Not one of us can accomplish this stuff working alone!"

Or

"My purpose is to see that we give more than lip service to what we say we value -- input from diverse viewpoints. There have been too many times when someone has come up with a whole different way of thinking about an issue that made disagreements disappear -- it is not possible for me not to try to get us to take whatever time we need to discuss this -- and I know we are under time pressure to act, but I think we are closer to core values by not rushing this vote."

There is no single right way to state your purposes so that their connectedness to your values is clear. But it is important to recognize that stating your purposes in such a way that others are still left with the question ". . . But for what purpose?" is the wrong way to do it. We assume that your values concerning the world -- and especially other people -- are at the minimum benign, and in most cases, affirming, protective, conserving, constructive, restorative or redemptive. However, not everyone knows to make such assumptions about you. Even people who know you well and know you are not a destructive, ruthless, self-aggrandizing, evil person will sometimes become wary or defensive because they are not sure what you are up to.

The more you can make your purposes clear by showing how they are anchored in your values and directed toward a future consistent with those values, the less people will need to protect themselves from you. The more you can link what you are tenaciously trying to make happen -- your purposes -- with the values that make it important to you, the less people will accuse you of being stubborn or over-reacting. The clearer you are that your purposes for acquiescing, accommodating or compromising are dictated by peace-making, bridging, healing, collaborating values, the less likely you will be dismissed as a nobody whose opinion does not matter.

Questioning yourself about your purposes is the best way to get your purposes and values connected. Ask yourself repeatedly, "for what purpose?", until the answer stops being, "in order to . . .", and becomes, "because I believe that is right or good!" For example, imagine you are about to deliver evaluative feedback to a colleague concerning his/her part in a team presentation to customers.

**The colleague says:** "Just skip the 'here are all the ways you were wonderful', and tell me what I need to work on!"

**You say to colleague:** "It's important to me to give you a balanced picture -- so I don't want to just tell you what needs to be improved."

If you ask yourself, *for what purpose do you want to give a balanced picture?*, the answer might be, "I don't feel right about just focusing on negatives."

So then shall we assume
your purpose is to feel
good?

"No, not entirely, but I give better feedback if I am not uncomfortable or feel something isn't right."

So then the purpose is for
you  to do a good job of
giving feedback.

"Yes, my purpose is to do a good job of giving feedback -- I believe it is very important -- and I would like to do it in a way that is most comfortable for both of us.  I believe that's the right way to do it."

**You say to colleague:**   "I want to do a good job of giving feedback -- I think it is very important -- and I would like to do it in a way that is most comfortable for both of us.  I believe that's the right way to do it. So if belaboring the positive feedback makes you uncomfortable and reporting only negative feedback makes me uncomfortable, my purpose is to find a compromise we can both live with."

We have labelled disconnecting your **purposes** from what should be their source -- namely your **values** -- and failing to disclose the **purposes ↔ values connection** as an impediment to effective communication at work. There are people who may still cling to the illusion that they can remain morally neutral in the midst of workplace transactions. They can be heard saying, *"I don't want to impose my values on others"*.

We are recommending that you become clearer about the connection between your values and your purposes and that you share that information with others. You are deluding yourself if you think you can suspend your biases, expectations and preconceptions and enter your workplace transactions completely open and value-free.

Anyone who has learned to think about human interactions using a particular language and who has learned to view human interactions through the lenses of a particular culture has a value-laden assumptive world concerning human interaction. The choice is **not** whether or not to have a value-laden assumptive world -- the choice is whether or not to know as much as you can about it. Especially important is the connection between your values and your purposes -- the  bridge over which you move from your value-laden assumptive world to the things you are trying to make happen -- moment-by-moment, as well as day-by-day and year-by-year.

In addition to unconnectedness between your purposes and your values being a barrier to effective communication at work, an entanglement of your purposes and methods for accomplishing your purposes can also block communication at work.

## Purposes ↔ Methods: Entangled

If you asked yourself or if you could inquire of others: "What is your purpose?" as you are in the midst of almost any interpersonal transaction at work, amazingly, more often than not an honest answer would be: "I'm not sure." When people are required to face the question "What impact am I trying to have -- what am I trying to make happen?", typically they have not thought about it very specifically -- they certainly are not consciously using active, intentional purposes to direct their performances.

In addition to such lack of proactive engagement among co-workers, we have also discussed how the lack of groundedness that results from failing to understand how your purposes connect with your values cripples communication at work.

Yet another barrier blocking communication at work is erected when the difference between a person's purposes and the methods for accomplishing them is not recognized. This is especially true when the person has mixed or multiple purposes that seem contradictory.

Consider the following two constructs:

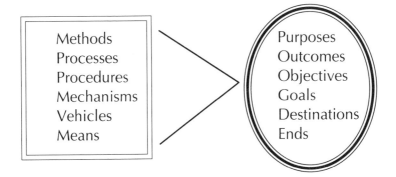

| Methods | Purposes |
| Processes | Outcomes |
| Procedures | Objectives |
| Mechanisms | Goals |
| Vehicles | Destinations |
| Means | Ends |

All of the terms in the oval target concern the same reality -- i.e., *where you are headed, but as yet have not reached.* All of the terms in the box concern *the way you will reach wherever you are headed.*

If you have power and authority in a work situation, you will be called upon to set limits, give directions, set the pace and make decisions often. You will need to know the difference between telling workers that **X** goal must be accomplished  -- **your purpose** -- but that they are free to do it any way that will get the job done -- **their methods**, compared to telling workers that not only must **X** be accomplished -- **your goal** -- but they must do it in exactly the manner you specify -- **your methods**.

Clearly, you need to realize the impact of your demanding that a person not only accept your purpose but also your methods, because typically, the imposition of methods is experienced as much more constraining. Your situation may require that you impose both method and purpose. If it is true that a person needs to comply precisely with your specifications as to how something should be accomplished, then by all means unilaterally, but humanely, impose your specifications. If there is a way to impose purpose and negotiate methods, that works better in most cases.

In a situation where you have less power, you may have decided to go along with a person in authority and facilitate whatever is that person's purpose. If the person in authority does not know the difference between purpose and method, you may receive a detailed set of instructions regarding how to proceed with something and not be told what the purpose of proceeding is. Or you may be given a clear statement of purpose -- an elaborate description of *what for* and *why,* but there may be no mention of *when to* or *how to.* If you know the difference between *where you are going -- purpose --* and *how to get there -- methods --* and if you can untangle the two by making clear what you do understand and what is still unclear, then you can avoid some major communication failures.

Few people realize how long it takes to clarify and agree upon mutually held purposes. It can be done, but it takes time and effort and communication skills. Any staff or committee or other task force which does not clarify purposes and agree on mutually held purposes before they allow themselves to discuss methods will function very inefficiently -- if at all.

Consider this all-too-common opening of a task force meeting. The emphasis is immediately on **how to do** the task before **what is the purpose** of the task is agreed upon.

| | |
|---|---|
| **Committee chair:** | "We need to decide how we're going to meet our 100% quota!" |
| **Committee member #1:** | "I don't think we should post people's names as to who donated how much." |
| **Committee member #2:** | "I agree, but I think it's fair to post and circulate the department contribution record." |
| **Committee member #3:** | "But some departments are so small -- there's only one person -- that's not fair. We shouldn't put that much pressure on anyone. These are supposed to be voluntary contributions." |

To avoid this fragmented discussion of what to do, the Committee Chair would have had to state purposes early and encourage people to delay talking about methods until purposes were clear. Compare the following discussion:

**Committee chair:** "I believe we need to address the the purpose of this committee and the purpose of the United Fund Drive before we discuss strategies."

**Committee member #1:** "I don't think we should post people's names as to who donated how much."

**Committee chair:** "I believe it is important to discuss such matters as how public or private to be about individual contributions, but first we need to agree on why we are doing this at all! What are our purposes? What do we hope to accomplish?"

The situation that divides people at work most often is one where somebody wants to do **X** -- someone else thinks **Y** would be better -- and they begin to debate and argue. Defensiveness is instantly high on both sides and although people remain outwardly civil, no one listens to anyone else. What these people do not find out until much later -- if at all -- is that the **X** method people and the **Y** method people had very compatible goals/purposes and the **X** and **Y** methods could easily have been carried out simultaneously or sequentially or in combination. Debating whether

*X* or *Y* is the superior method was totally unnecessary.

The doorway to effective problem solving with two or more people opens wide after individuals have clarified their purposes and agreed upon a mutually held set of purposes. It is important that you not entangle purpose and method in your thinking. In a work setting transaction, you must be able to tell the difference between and label accurately people's purpose statements and their method statements.

Even more importantly, you must be able to monitor whether you are making a purpose statement -- *what for* -- or a method statement -- *how to*. For example, suppose you are facing an evaluation session wherein you expect you will be criticized for some events in the office that were not entirely your fault. You, of course, would be well served to have proactively considered the up-coming meeting and clarified your purposes and the values from which they spring. You might have discovered that your purposes are:

1  to listen skillfully and make it clear you
   understand your evaluator's position

2  to remain calm and non-defensive as you
   state your explanation and assessment of
   the office events.

3  to accept full responsibility for your part in
   the office difficulties, but to avoid having
   more than your  fair share of the trouble
   attributed to you.

4  to accept and/or develop ways to cope with
   the situation now and in the future.

Whether you state your purposes at the very beginning of the evaluation session or wait until you have paraphrased your evaluator's opening remarks does not change your purposes. Whether you use humor to cope with your anxiety in the situation or whether you remain deadly serious, does not change your purposes. At some point early in the interaction, you will probably be well-served to state your purposes. For example, you might say:

> "My purposes are to hear and understand the situation from your point of view, describe how I see things and see what we can figure out is best to do now. I want very much to accept full responsibility for my part, but of course I want to be fair to myself at the same time."

Whether you and your evaluator can accomplish all this in one session or you will need to meet more than once does not change your purposes. Focusing on your purposes, rather than how they will be accomplished, and stating them aloud, rather than leaving them rattling around in your head where only you hear them, keep you from getting your purposes entangled with methods for achieving them. You avoid the reactive posture and defensiveness heard in this sort of thinking:

> "...I better get a chance to have my side heard ... I'm sure not going to take all the blame for this ... I don't want to be defensive, but ...I wonder what has already been said ..."

When you make clear what your purposes are by using positive proactive language -- stating what you would like to see happen -- having already linked those purposes to your values -- even though you may have identified a complex mixture of purposes -- you are more likely to keep your purposes and the methods for accomplishing them clear and unentangled. When that is the case, you can perform all forms of communication at work more effectively.

We turn now to consider factors which can interfere with a variety of human performances -- but which also have the potential to elevate a performance to the level of brilliance. Since we are focused on understanding deterrents to excellent communication at work, we will discuss flawed, rather than fantastic, rhythm and timing.

## Rhythm and Timing: Inappropriate

On the one hand, this impediment to communication at work is very easily specified: your rhythm and timing are off! What could be more elementary than informing folks that the reason they are having difficulty communicating at work is not because they are failing to plan proactively, not because they are failing to connect their purposes and values and not because they have their purposes and methods entangled -- but because their rhythm and timing are inappropriate.

Some examples follow:

1   at a time when the most appropriate response to a situation is to take a stand -- declare yourself -- aggressively step up to meet it -- the person who suffers with this communication block chooses to be aquiescent and/or noncommittal.

2   at a point where anyone with good sense would

-- let go, step away -- the person who suffers with this communication block chooses to continue assertively trying to negotiate a mutually agreeable compromise.

3   on an occasion when everyone present is moving more slowly, talking more quietly, focusing on serious rather than frivolous matters, because of what is happening -- the person who suffers with this communication block is flitting about, chatting with old friends and talking about fun things to do.

On the other hand, this communication stumbling block is the most difficult to deal with: what do you say to folks who appear not to be able to *track* what's happening around them?  How do you encourage individuals who appear to be unable to *read* a situation, anticipate what is likely to happen next and use their perceptions as a basis for how they choose to perform?

The first step they need to take is to be able to describe their own poor rhythm and timing and explain how such performance difficulties might have developed. They also need to understand how poor timing and inappropriate rhythm are workplace liabilities and identify when and where they are more likely to be a problem.

Drawing a parallel between job performance and dramatic performance is helpful to some folks who struggle with this communication block.  We are, of course, concerned about improving people's job performance.  We are not trying to make actors or dancers or singers out of our readers, but there is a striking similarity in the two performance situations.  Sometimes we will use the dramatic metaphor as if you were a member of an audience viewing a drama unfolding before you; sometimes the metaphor will have you on stage actually participating in the dramatic action. Throughout, our purpose will be to clarify the difficulties associated with poor timing and inappropriate rhythm.

Inexperienced actors move about on stage, often in a manner that communicates that they do not know *upstage* from *downstage, stage right* from *stage left* and that they may not be clear on the difference it makes whether something happens *center stage* or on the *apron.* Translating this metaphor to your work situation, if you do not know up from down, if you cannot in a staff meeting keep track of central vs. peripheral issues and actions, then you can hardly expect to be taken seriously. On stage, it looks amateurish; on the job, it looks naive.

Not only do you need to be familiar with the stage itself, but you must also have a clear sense of the set actually being what it was designed to represent -- whether that be an 18th century European drawing room or an open field in Montana. When you move about comfortably on stage or on the job, you communicate a relaxed competence that is reassuring to others. If you are unfamiliar, uncomfortable or feel unnatural in your surroundings, you will move about and relate to people in uncomfortable, unnatural ways that will typically be viewed as arrogance or incompetence or both.

**Rhythm** as you move about the space within which you function and **timing** as you interact with the things in those settings are both important. Both rhythm and timing are especially important as you interact with the people in your world. The more we learn about our world -- from sub-atomic particles to the neuropsychology of the planet's most significant occupants -- namely humans -- to the global eco-system -- the more we recognize the importance of the *patterns that connect*. The more we understand about applications of *chaos theory*, the easier it is to appreciate the importance of patterns. People who cannot seem to feel workplace rhythms and who do not seem to have a sense of timing at work, have greater difficulties contributing to and enjoying a team approach to the workplace. Rhythm and timing greatly affect routine communication at work.

## Examples of rhythm and timing problems:

---

### #1

You are hosting an open house in your office for the holiday season. You are the person who must function as facilitator, social mobilizer, overseer of the human interactions, the consumption of refreshments and the traffic flow. A manager from another office who is above you in status and power, walks up, stands too close, begins talking business and obviously intends to take whatever time is required to discuss the several issues which this manager believes are important. You cannot carry out your hosting responsibilities under the circumstances. Some people have incredibly poor timing socially. They do not seem to understand the role demands and the rhythm of responsibilities for others.

---

---

#### #2

You are waiting for your turn for a duplicating machine. You are delighted to find out there is only one person in front of you, but disappointed when you find out who it is. You have seen before how this particular individual seems to have no sense of how machines work -- paper is fed in too quickly, the *on* button is pressed too soon, telephone numbers are punched faster than they can register, the car is easily flooded, etc. Some people have very poor rhythm and timing with machines. They do not seem to *understand* machines.

---

#### #3

Your healthy, vibrant, energetic, 60 year old boss has just this week been turned down on a lateral transfer. Only one month ago, the boss's request for funds to attend a training program being actively promoted by Central Office was also turned down. Your boss is rapidly reaching the conclusion that early retirement is being pushed as the most attractive route to take. In the break room, a person has been telling horror stories about the negative effects of retirement -- stroke, heart attack, depression, early senility, etc. -- when the boss walks in. The storyteller proceeds as if oblivious to the impact of the topic. In fact, at the end of this last tragic tale, the storyteller turns to the boss and says, "I guess you will have to watch it -- you're not far from retirement, right?"

## In contrast, consider this example of smooth timing:

You are driving a co-worker's car from one part of the plant to a parking lot two miles away. The fastest route is on a freeway. You start the unfamiliar car, judge what pickup it has, how responsive and easily controlled it is as you leave the parking area and approach the freeway on-ramp. As you near where the freeway and the service road intersect, you look and sense the movement of traffic on the freeway. A space opens and you move smoothly into it, appreciating the truck driver who changed lanes to make that easier for you. You could sense the rhythm of the traffic and could anticipate the car's movement in the freeway traffic -- how it would feel -- even before you entered the traffic. The transition, therefore, was well-timed and very smooth.

In all four examples, whether we are talking about machines or people, an empathic understanding and anticipatory sense of the impact you probably will have is evident in the well-timed, rhythmic response. If a person does not have a general sense of how things and/or people function, awkwardness in both people/machine interactions and people/people transactions is typical. If when growing up, the person never developed rhythm and timing for daily living, it is very difficult to acquire them late in life.

Inappropriate rhythm and timing can certainly be a major stumbling block to communication at work. Some people simply do not intuitively sense the speed with which -- cars, bikes, dogs, sunsets, conversations, negotiations -- are moving. They have trouble distinguishing what is central vs. peripheral or whether *later* would be better than *now*. It is difficult for those people to anticipate and select which combination of communication tools would be most fitting to use in particular situations. A person could be competent in executing separate communication skills and yet possess such poor rhythm and inappropriate timing that the effectiveness of even the three **NEM2 MasterSkills**® [presented in Chapter 5] is significantly reduced.

The final barrier blocking communication at work which we will consider is expectations about performance -- your own and others' -- that are unreasonable.

## Performance expectations:  Unreasonable

Sometimes people in the workplace expect too much of themselves and others when it comes to performance and sometimes they expect too little. Either of these erroneous ways of viewing yourself and/or others can distort and limit communication at work.

Before we examine the most common expectation errors in the workplace, we need to clarify some faulty assumptions that are a set-up for people to feel ashamed of their performances. More than a few people feel indicted and convicted by the message: *you only use about 10% of your potential!* People actually suffer with the judgment that they are wasting about 90% of their capacity.

"If you only tried harder, you could . . ." You could what? Add hours to your day or days to your life span? Obviously not! You could what? Be more efficient and be two places or three places at once? Obviously not!  Regardless of how talented and competent you are, there are only 24 hours in a day and you can only be in one place at a time. Time and space are real existential limits that will not change -- no matter what skills you acquire.

In contrast, we can honestly say there is virtually no limit to your learning new skills, new information, new ways to view your experiences and new insights regarding yourself. Most of us could learn better ways to organize our time, manage our responsibilities and accomplish more in the time we have available. But to learn such skills and information, we would have to be taught. It is not a matter of trying harder. The reason that you and others fail to make maximum efficient use of your time is not a matter of insufficient motivation, it is a matter of not having the information and skills to set up a fail-safe, time management program.

Humans *do not inherit* very many skills, but humans do inherit the equipment to learn. Humans are born with very little information and ability, but humans are *hard-wired to acquire* an enormous range and amount of understanding and skill throughout their lives. If you believe people need to be *motivated* to learn, ask yourself what you mean. It is very **natural** for people to learn.

It is true that people need to feel safe -- physically and psychologically -- when they are trying to learn because they have had many experiences that taught them that learning almost always requires making mistakes. If you are trying to facilitate another person's learning, you do not need to *motivate* the learner; you need to engage the learner in an interactive process with you and/or others involving something of value. It is important for the learner to know it is **safe** to make mistakes.

If you are trying to facilitate your own learning, you do not need to *motivate* yourself, you just need to be certain your learning circumstances are safe, participative, interactive, competence building and worthy of your time and effort. Under these conditions, **learning occurs naturally**.

Consider this: you would not berate yourself for failing to speak a foreign language you have never been taught. You would not criticize yourself and tell yourself, *"If you only tried harder you could speak Japanese."* Why, then, do you criticize yourself and others for failing to do things that neither you nor they were ever taught to do? You probably could design a perfect learning situation within which you would learn Japanese very naturally. You could also design a perfect learning context within which you and others would naturally learn the skills that make constructive communication at work a reasonable expectation. Unfortunately, very few people you know -- probably including you -- will have spent much time in such a set of circumstances designed especially to provide a learning context where communication skills for the workplace could be learned naturally.

The following list of human behaviors we have taught to people of all ages -- 5 years old to 75 years old -- to people whose circumstances vary tremendously -- rich to poor -- to people of differing ability levels -- brilliant to dull -- as well as to people in all parts of the world -- thatched huts on tiny islands in the Pacific to elegant offices in the heart of London.

**This is a list of interpersonal skills which most people have never been consistently exposed to growing up nor directly taught by a coach who saw they had a safe place to practice, but which most people expect they and others should somehow possess and use regularly:**

- controlling breathing and body tension while being verbally attacked
- strongly disagreeing without ridiculing the other person
- continuing to problem solve after being insulted
- stopping an authority to state that you do not believe that you have been heard
- willingly, graciously stepping over and ignoring an inappropriate comment
- remaining centered in the face of sarcasm
- giving another person clear, positive reinforcement
- complimenting a superior without being manipulative
- directing an interview without being overbearing
- increasing the intensity of an interaction
- decreasing the intensity of an interaction
- talking to yourself in constructive, encouraging ways
- inviting others to risk sharing their thoughts
- instructing another person on how s/he could be encouraging to you
- inviting others to assist you plan
- giving corrective feedback constructively
- calming a person who is furiously angry
- refusing to be questioned when the purpose is unclear
- resisting coercive pressure to comply when you prefer to do otherwise
- warning a person that you are becoming angry and will either leave or become hostile unless the process can be turned around
- setting up a self improvement program
- describing to a safe, trusted person that you are nervous or scared about something
- offering to be helpful, when it is not clear if helping is even possible
- inquiring about the well-being of a friend or colleague in a genuine manner
- telling interesting stories in a small group
- making it easy for people to serve you
- overcoming irrational fears and phobias
- *paraphrasing*
- *purpose stating*
- *performance imaging*

Everything on the list could be learned by almost everyone. However, if a person has not been directly taught or if a person did not grow up with a clear, consistent example of the behavior which could be observed frequently, then do not **expect** that a person has mastered the skill.

It is true that this list could go on and on or we might cluster many of the behaviors under headings such as : remaining non-defensive, being clear and honest, engaging in self-improvement, etc. and make the list smaller. However, such headings usually result in people thinking of the items as matters of motivation -- **will** problems -- rather than behavior performance competence -- **skill** problems.

Let us say again, very likely you could learn to do everything on the list if you were taught to do so. Making up your mind and trying harder will not teach you how to do things differently. It is fine to remind yourself that your capacity to learn new things is practically limitless. However, do not slip into telling yourself that if you tried harder you could be 90% more effective or that somehow you could eliminate the existential boundaries constraining all of us.

## Performance expectation errors; expecting too little

Expecting too little of a supervisor, co-worker or supervisee usually results in closing down, discouraging, short circuiting or diminishing potential for cooperation and collaboration. Because we expect so little, we do not even attempt to work together. Diminished expectations produce diminishing returns. What follows is an example of a supervisor who *did no*t make expectation errors.

**Supervisor/Manager:**

"My purpose in asking for a conference with you, David, was to present not only a set of tasks I want you to do, but also the context for the assignment. I am feeling vulnerable and over-reactive about this project. My boss wanted to assign it to a different department, but his boss said "no". She has seen some of my work that is comparable to this project and was impressed and specifically said she wanted the project given to us. I'm not sure my boss knows that I know all that -- I heard it indirectly, but from someone who heard the discussion between the two of them. Obviously none of this should be told in any form.

On top of this, the woman with whom I live teaches school and has my boss's grandson in her 3rd grade class. The youngster has been having some difficulty and my boss has put a lot of pressure on his daughter-in-law to make the school do its job. Again, I am in no position to discuss this either and I don't know what he thinks I know. He knows Jackie and I live together.

The last thing is that this particular project includes procedures which I personally developed, and the last company I was with marketed them without my permission and without my receiving any credit. So I have very mixed feelings about the whole thing. I know I need to delegate this project because of my schedule, but it will be hard for me to leave it alone."

With a context description such as this, a worker would have a much better understanding of why the supervisor/ manager might be more vigilant than necessary, nervous about the project's success and reluctant to leave it alone. Now the two of them can joke lightly about the degree of *bird dogging* by the supervisor/manager.

There are very few people who when given the whole story -- positive and negative, weak and strong, sound and self-defeating, petty and profound -- would fail to view the situation appropriately. If you tell people they need to be discrete and why they need to be discrete -- if you level with them rather than deny or distort the facts -- the vast majority of workers would handle the situation appropriately. Too often we expect too little, share too little and receive very little from a worker who could have produced much more with adequate information, clear guidelines and some encouragement.

This same principle applies to your superiors. Rather than telling yourself that your supervisor/manager really does not care and would not want to be bothered with you, assume that s/he wants to be competent as a supervisor, which means attending to and encouraging you.

If you expect very little from your supervisor in the way of consulting, supervising, facilitating, intervening, as well as constructive evaluation, you will likely receive very little. Obviously, if you are mindlessly *bugging* your boss, asking ridiculous questions, wanting approval for every little thing, then you should expect a disapproving response. However, if you expect more and learn the skills necessary to non-demandingly make your purposes known -- you can expect that nine out of ten supervisor/managers will welcome your regular approaches.

In the following example, a supervisee does not allow *expecting too little of the supervisor* to interfere with creating an opportunity to collaborate:

| | |
|---|---|
| **Supervisee:** | "The reason I arranged for some of your time this morning is that I'm about to start in on the annual report and each time I go through this I get so worried and upset about it . . . " |
| **Supervisor:** | "Well, of course it's a pretty important task you're doing." |
| **Supervisee:** | "So maybe I'm not all that far off . . . It's pretty important!" |
| **Supervisor:** | "Yes, but I think you are too hard on yourself and become unnecessarily upset about it." |
| **Supervisee:** | "So do I! That's why I wanted to talk. . . because I think I know what would cut down on some of that . . . I would like to schedule ten minutes of your time every day you are here to go over what I have done to date." |
| **Supervisor:** | "Ten minutes everyday doesn't seem realistic. Fifteen minutes every few days seems more reasonable." |
| **Supervisee:** | "I'm not trying to get you to do the job or approve of my every move, but I know I could eliminate some of the ridiculous self talk about how my writing is awful, terrible and completely out in left field." |
| **Supervisor:** | "Of course, in fifteen minutes I can't give a thorough, studied assessment of your project." |

| | |
|---|---|
| **Supervisee:** | "That's not what I need. I would benefit from just making brief, regular contact while I'm immersed in it...plus, I'm confident that if something were really weird or off target, you or I would very likely spot it." |
| **Supervisor:** | "I'm not here a lot . . ." |
| **Supervisee:** | "I'm sure I would get what I needed from a brief contact every few days. I'll take full responsibility for making it happen and I don't see your being in and out of the office a problem. I just need to check in when you are here." |
| **Supervisor:** | "Well, that's fine with me... and if that will make the annual report go easier for you, I'd be really happy to talk with you." |
| **Supervisee:** | "Thanks, I'll see to it this doesn't become a big burden. It will be a *progress report*, not a *lack of progress report.* |

Clearly, ***expecting too little of others*** impedes communication at work and blocks collaborative problem solving -- why bother being collaborative or trying to solve problems with people you view as too stupid, too egocentric, too lazy or too uncommitted to reciprocate? It is not uncommon for a person -- supervisor or line worker -- who expects very little that is positive, to fall into cynicism and even become passive aggressive toward the entire workplace.

Hopefully, it is also clear that if a person expects helpful, cooperative, thoughtful, intelligent responses from a supervisor, co-worker or supervisee and skillfully uses a combination of constructive communication skills, the probability is greatly increased that effective communication at work will occur.

## Performance expectation errors; expecting too much

Our introductory remarks about erroneous expectations warned against the horrible berating of self and others in which many people engage . Even in cases where it is true that you knew better and did not try hard enough, ripping self criticism rarely -- if ever -- is constructive. It is helpful to face up to one's shortcomings, feel ashamed and guilty and then move on to a constructive plan for remedying the situation. Wallowing in remorse, immersing oneself in waves of guilt and shame, tearing at oneself with barbed self-evaluations are not useful ways to handle any situation -- even one that we could all agree was a terrible mess and you caused it!

However, before you allow even a moderate amount of guilt induction and shaming, be certain that you were not expecting too much. If you never learned how to do whatever you are insisting you should have done, then it is unreasonable to expect you could do it. This same position applies, of course, to your expecting others to do things they have never learned to do. Severe disapproval of someone else is also unlikely to produce a desired result.

You and others may be capable of skillfully executing a tremendous number of work-related activities, some of them may be very difficult tasks. It is reasonable to expect you will perform them, providing, of course, that:

1  you have been taught how to do so
2  you have sufficient structure/support
3  you have not been heavily punished for proactivity

It is also unreasonable to expect that you will carry through -- for example, develop new procedures, present a project, negotiate with another department, recruit volunteers, investigate an accident, etc. -- even if you know how, when there is not sufficient structure to support the effort. Human beings do not function well in a vacuum. They require visible supportive structures within which and by means of which they function. Memos, models, mission statements, written game plans, progress charts, benchmarks, letters of appreciation, bonuses, incentives, retreats away from the workplace, titles, briefing sessions, debriefing sessions, staff meetings, newsletters, conference calls, conference rooms -- are some of the means by which humans structure and support their activities.

There is not a precise formula specifying the exact amount of structuring and support required to keep you going, but there is a minimum level below which you cannot reasonably be expected to function. Telling yourself to *carry on* because -- after all -- the process should be rewarding or the product is a real thrill is rarely sufficient. *Carrying on* with most work tasks requires some support and structure from other human beings as well as tangible rewards. The acknowledgement may be small, the conference brief, the written material in outline form only, but something needs to be exchanged with another person. If you are expecting that you or others can perform without such recognition/support, you are expecting too much.

In trying to judge how much to expect from yourself and others, you must also consider the possibility that you or others have been punished in the past for being proactive -- initiative taking, eagerness and a focus on possibilities may have resulted in insults and even reprimands. Burn-out is a known phenomenon in many job situations -- in the human service areas it is especially acute. If you have been through the mill -- eager, hopeful optimism ground down to depleted, defeated pessimism -- about making changes in systems and institutions which could put an end to the ridiculous wasteful self defeating programs we keep pursuing -- then you know about burn-out. If you have struggled long and hard to extricate a client from a damaging situation -- drug addition, alcoholism, compul-sive gambling, a battering partner, chronic unemploy-ment, prostitution, etc. -- only to have that client choose to return to the old, familiar life style after a month of being *free*, then you know about burn-out.

Before you allow yourself to criticize and chastise a co-worker's failure to show initiative, make an investment and take risks, be certain that you are not expecting too much. If a person burned out on the last *set of challenges* -- if a person was punished for caring and investing so much -- if there was insufficient structure and support and/ or if the person was expected to do things for which there was no training, then do not be surprised if that person is much more self-protective this time.

Before you can reasonably expect people to work posi-tively, energetically, creatively and independently, they need to know they have a sufficient support structure and adequate skills. If you are in a supervisory role you may be able to make that happen for the person. If you are being supervised by a burned out person, you may need to tell of your willingness to be counted on for support, planning and problem solving -- if it is appropriate.

To keep performance expectation errors -- expecting too much of yourself and others -- from creeping into your judgments, develop several methods of self-inquiry. For example:

- Ask yourself how a dozen, reasonably intelligent adults drawn randomly from your vicinity would view your expectations.

- Ask a trusted colleague/friend whose judgment you respect to evaluate your expectations.

- Ask yourself to project five years into the future and look back at the item about which you have expectations and comment from that distant perspective.

The fact that you are genuinely concerned about and committed to avoiding having an unreasonably high set of performance expectations for both yourself and others provide the best safe guards against such errors interfering with communication at work.

# Communication at Work

# Chapter 4

# Coaching *communication at work*

## The name of the game has changed

Surviving the 90's and thriving in the Third Millennium require doing business differently. Business managers and supervisors across the nation are being told to share information and resources across boundaries, to establish a *customer perspective* within their teams and departments, to create an atmosphere of *continuous learning* and to engage all workers in *participating meaningfully* in improving the workplace. **Business management must change -- rapidly and radically.**

**What must change is no mystery!** A growing world-wide emphasis on human rights and democratization means that the *workforce will become more empowered.* With cross-cultural business alliances increasing weekly, we must *celebrate diversity* and learn to work collaboratively. With increasingly limited resources, *we will do more with less.*

> **What must change is the way we manage the only unlimited resource we have -- the value-adding capacity of the workforce.**

The most frequently referred to method for accomplishing such change is **TQM** -- Total Quality Management -- or **CQI** -- Continuous Quality Improvement.

**Who must change is no mystery!** TQM/CQI requires commitment from the top down; that is the first and easiest step. Increasingly, top management in both private and public sector organizations has sufficient vision to see that implementing TQM/CQI philosophy and practices is not optional -- it is essential.

We know that empowered employees working together with empowered managers implementing changes in the organization's structure and procedures results in value-added productivity and service. We know that employees closest to the delivery of a service or the manufacture of a product are best equipped to identify needed improvements.

Workers closest to the line -- line of fire, hot line, line of goods, production line, etc. -- easily understand the importance of implementing TQM/CQI philosophy and procedures. Research has consistently shown that when their opinions matter to management, when they are listened to and understood by supervisors, when they feel safe speaking their thoughts, when they are able to exercise some control over their work lives, when they are actively and skillfully engaged in the ongoing workplace change process -- that is, when they are empowered -- line workers thrive and productivity soars.

Continuing to be a player in the new economy workplace is not something a middle manager/ supervisor can take for granted. Middle managers have become a threatened species almost overnight. Only those supervisors who can coach and empower are value-adding to a company. TQM/CQI requires that managers function as coaches to the people they serve; this is the most difficult step an organization must take to implement TQM/CQI.

Many middle managers find knowing where to stand or what to do very difficult. The managers in the middle -- in the now out-dated, hierarchical/industrial organization -- have been defined as those above line supervisors, but below senior managers. As reformulated by Stan Davis in **Future Perfect**, 1987,

". . . it is more effective to think of people in the middle as those who have direct responsibility for the user-provider relationship, regardless of where they are in the hierarchy. These people are truly in the middle, that is, in the middle of the customer-employee relationship in the business, rather than in the middle of the employee-employee hierarchy in the organization." p. 79

These workers in the middle have thus far experienced the greatest struggle with translating TQM/CQI into action.

At every turn, now, we hear -- the supervisor of the future is a coach. No more command/control autocratic leadership. Coaching is *how* supervision should be done. Empowerment is *what* supervision/coaching is supposed to do and, of course, teams of workers are who the coaching is to benefit. Manager/supervisors -- especially those is the middle -- within organizations of all sizes must learn to **empower through coaching** the people who report to them if we are to step up to and meet 21st Century challenges.

> **We believe the heart of empowerment is coaching communication skills -- from the top, in the middle or on the line.**

As we grapple with understanding how the game has changed in the workplace, James P. Carse helps us understand a very valuable distinction discussed in his small book, **Finite and Infinite Games**, *1985.*

> "There are at least two kinds of games.
> One could be called finite, the other infinite.
>
> A finite game is played for the purpose of winning, an infinite game for the purpose of continuing the play." *p. 3*
>
> "Finite games can be played within an infinite game, but an infinite game cannot be played within a finite game.
>
> "Infinite players regard their wins and losses in whatever finite games they play as but moments in continuing play." *p. 7*

Coaching for empowerment in the workplace means something different than it would have meant just a few years ago. A necessary part of what it means -- in fact the heart of the matter -- is coaching communication at work.

Further discussion of the fundamental changes in the nature of work and the workplace appears in Chapter 6.

The remainder of this chapter will present *coaching communication at work* by attending to the following:

- **Creating coachable moments**
- **Coaching by example**
- **Coaching by encouraging**
- **Coaching by education**
- **Coaching by empowering**

## Creating coachable moments

Most people reading this book will have been coached or will have been a coach in one or another performance arena -- sports, music, public speaking, dance, etc. Such experience may help a person who intends to coach for empowerment in the workplace to better understand the role *coach.* For example, coaches perform from the sidelines or backstage in contrast to on the field or center-stage. Having been a *star* does very little to prepare a performer to be a coach and, in fact, may interfere. Having been the star salesperson or the finest production person does not prepare a person to coach others. In contrast, experience coaching in other performance arenas is more likely to help prepare a manager/supervisor for empowerment coaching in the workplace.

When they are asked to describe a *coach,* people emphasize different aspects of the role -- some focus on the coach being inspiring and motivating -- some point to teaching/training/drilling/rehearsing as the most important part of the role -- some view strategic management of the coached performance as most important. Everyone agrees, however, that facilitating excellent performances by those they coach is the coach's essential purpose.

Facilitating excellent performances by those they super-vise in the workplace is what a supervisor/coach must do. It is easy to conjure up pictures of a supervisor/manager coaching by facilitating the worker's performance with a piece of equipment, or filling out a form, or estimating costs. These images are valid and what they depict is important. However, the most important skills that need to be facilitated -- coached to perfection -- are communi-cation skills.

Picture yourself or another manager/supervisor coaching workers on communication at work by preparing a person to lead a meeting more effectively, listen to the anger of a fellow team member without becoming defensive, re-quest assistance without sounding autocratic, give cor-rective feedback to a team member without demeaning the person, register dissatisfaction with another depart-ment, etc. Coaching people you supervise on how to skillfully execute these situations and hundreds similar to them would truly facilitate excellence in their work per-formance.

Chapter 5 presents the necessary and sufficient **NEM2 MasterSkills®** required to effectively communicate at work. What needs to be noted here is that if you are a supervisor/manager of others, then you need to coach them on their people skills just as much if not more than on their technical skills. Waiting until they come to you for help will not work. Offering a standing invitation, "If you need help, just let me know" or "My door is always open", is useless. The only way coaching communication at work will take place is if you -- the coach -- **create coachable moments**.

**Example #1**  Having seen a new team member become visibly agitated by the way an older, more experienced worker gives feedback, you -- the supervisor/coach -- say to the younger/ newest person, in private:

> "I have observed what I believe is an unpleasant experience for you -- namely Don giving you feedback -- and I would like to talk with you about it because I think I could coach you on some ways to make that easier on yourself. . . it doesn't have to be right now, but I'd like us to talk about it."

Having said the above, you have **created a coachable moment** -- now, or at some agreed upon time in the future.

**Example #2**  Having heard someone close down a telephone conversation with no effort to serve the customer -- even though it sounds as if the customer had the wrong department -- you, the supervisor/coach say to this person:

> " I overheard your half of the conversation as I was walking by and was troubled that your tone was not as helpful as I believe we need to sound . . .so I would like to discuss it with you. . .doesn't have to be now -- but soon I would like to review with you

> how you believe you communicate a
> general helpfulness over the phone. ..
> I will be happy to coach you on vari-
> ous ways I know it can be done."

Both of these examples do nothing more than **create a coachable moment**. They must be followed by actual coaching -- but you, the coach, have taken the first step.

Effectively coaching communication at work is not a lengthy process; it occurs in relatively small chunks of time. Once the people you supervise/manage have a grip on the three **NEM2 MasterSkills®** you can coach them on their use of these skills rather quickly and easily. This may be reminiscent of advice from the **One Minute Manager**, 1981, by Blanchard and Johnson that has been -- and continues to be -- a great help to managers/supervisors. Coaching communication at work could be carried out by using the philosophy and procedures of the **One Minute Manager**, provided you understand that it is your responsibility to **create coachable moments** and it is necessary that you and those you coach have at least least a beginning grasp of the **NEM2 MasterSkills®**.

## Coaching by example

There are many instances when a coach is not as able to execute the performance s/he is coaching as well as the person being coached -- for example, ballet, football, voice, golf, acting, basketball, etc. However, when it comes to coaching communication at work, the very nature of managing and supervising demands that the manager/ supervisor be an expert in communication at work. That means you are competent with and regularly use the **NEM2 MasterSkills**®.

In addition to being an exemplar of **NEM2 MasterSkills**® usage, effectively coaching communication at work also requires that by word and deed you make it clear to those you coach that you believe it is in your and their long term best interest to assume:

1  **Each person is doing the best that s/he can do at the moment.**

2  **Each person is unique.**

3  **Individuals have a great deal in common.**

4  **Individuals are not out to get you -- it is natural for humans to cooperate, help and share.**

5  **Constructive communication is demanding and difficult.**

6  **Improving your communication skills is certainly possible but it probably will not be easy.**

7  **Interpersonal transactions cannot be reduced to lifeless communication formulations.**

**Coaching by example** does not mean that you expect people to *pick-up people skills* only by watching you. It does mean you expect your behavior will not give those you coach a bad example to have to ignore.

# Coaching by encouraging

When we consider the word *encourage,* our first realization is that we are dealing with matters of the heart. The heart of the word *encourage* is the French word *couer* -- meaning *heart. To encourage* means to give confidence, hope or courage to. . .to embolden. . .to hearten. . .to inspire . . .to promote the growth of others.

The most encouraging messages a performer can hear from his/her coach is what and how the coach would like to work with the performer on improving his/her performance. "There are flaws in your performance that I want to see you eliminate or improve upon and I'm willing to work with you. . ." is not a discouraging message; it is an optimistic, growth promoting, *can do* message. Critical remarks designed to improve performance are basically an affirmation of the performer's worth and a testimony to the coach's commitment. Receiving constructive feedback about performance is essential for the performer's continued development. The following guidelines are designed to eliminate unnecessarily harsh or vague information from passing as constructive feedback.

## Constructive Feedback Guidelines

Receiving valid, reliable feedback about your performance presented in clear behavioral terms can be a great benefit for improving your performance. Receiving inaccurate and unskillfully presented feedback may be experienced as anything from a nuisance to a devastating attack. The ideal combination of objective feedback from video tape and an interpretive evaluation from an expert trainer

-- a coach -- mixed together with the comments of peers presenting their own observations create an enormous opportunity for participants to see and hear themselves as others do. Such self knowledge can be a profound break-through to improving performance.

---

**See yourself as others see you.**

**Hear yourself as others hear you.**

**Be impacted by your performance the way others are impacted by you.**

---

If video feedback and expert trainer evaluations are not immediately available, team members can critique their own performances and coach each other in ways that are very instructive. It is necessary to be respectful, objective and honest -- the way a camcorder treats you. When teams function in this very positive, constructive, practical way, they can appropriately be called *learning transfer teams.*

In order to be of maximum benefit to your fellow learning transfer team members or to those you coach:

1  First clarify what you understand the purposes of the performer's efforts to be -- that is, state what you think the person was trying to do.

2  Use behavior descriptions and feeling descriptions to distinguish your observations from your feelings when you present your feedback.

3  Focus on and report positive aspects of the person's performance first. Describe the ways the person successfully realized his/her purposes.

4  Then describe behavior which needs to be improved in clear behavioral terms. You may speculate about the impact of the person's behavior on others. You may state directly the impact on you. You may or may not be able to suggest what a person could do instead of what the person did. It is **not** necessary to be able to *fix it.*

5  Restate the more positive parts of the person's performance.

6  Tell the person to whom you are giving feedback that it is important to you to have been clear and constructive and you would appreciate a summary of your comments.

If you are faithful to these guidelines, there is very little you could not say to co-workers about their performances. That is not license to be cruel, but rather an invitation to be frank. The most destructive problems in the workplace -- concerning communication at work -- are the *unspeakable problems.*

Each of us knows what a relief it is when something awful, lurking in the shadows, has a bright light focused on it and the result is that whoever is holding the light does not shrink back in horror, but instead, moves in closer to see how the situation might be improved. The most encouraging news from a supervisor/coach is "I do not believe X is so horrible, that I can't discuss it with you. . .I believe X is something we can improve upon."

What follows is a list of flaws, problems, bad habits, short-comings, etc., that a coach could help with -- if they could be openly and directly discussed.  The items on this list are some communication at work problems that are typically relegated to the *unmentionable* pile.  They are all communication flaws that are correctable -- with some assistance -- but which will probably never improve on their own. All it would take is a supervisor/coach -- ***creating a coachable moment*** -- knowing that the person being coached will find it encouraging to be working with the coach on ways to improve communication at work.

**Communication problems that people are usually reluctant to identify and discuss -- even when they have supervisory/coaching responsibilty**:

Mispronunciation of common words
Distracting hand gestures
Nervous sounding laugh
Voice volume too great
Repeated interrupting
Overuse of filler phrases,e.g., "you know"
Too lengthy explanations
Sexist, racist, ageist terms
Immature sounding speech
Avoidance of eye contact
Looking around while supposedly listening
Starting to argue before understanding issues
Overuse of humor

No one would take a position that a person whose inter-actions were characterized by anything on the above list was doing so intentionally. No one wants to put others off by such distracting habits. It can be very encouraging to work with a supervisor/coach who is willing to speak openly and directly about such matters.

In addition to being willing to identify any behavior that interferes with communicating in the workplace as some-thing a person could improve, coaching by encouraging also means listening carefully for the meaning in what may sound like a meaningless point. People usually have something they regard as significant in mind when they speak. A coach known to have an encouraging impact on others is slow to discredit or dismiss what may have been presented in an awkward manner. Rather than become impatient with the garbled message, the coach/supervisor who understands coaching communication skills by encouragement sees an opportunity to **create a coachable moment.** Rather than become impatient, the encouraging coach/supervisor becomes *puzzled.*

Adopting a **posture of puzzlement** allows the coach/ supervisor time to picture what the worker is trying to communicate. Your remaining puzzled -- not jumping to conclusions in an effort to make sense out of what may not be immediately obvious -- engages the speaker in an effort to clarify further. The **posture of puzzlement** requires a tolerance for ambiguity and a degree of patience that are difficult for many supervisors. However, when coaches/ supervisors remain clear about their own purpose -- to coach communication at work by encouraging the people they supervise -- they are able to make inquiry without interrogating, to confess confusion without ridiculing and to help clarify without silencing the very people they are trying to engage and encourage.

Experiencing the coach's patient ***posture of puzzlement*** encourages team members to try being clear about their purposes, but patient in listening to one another which, of course, facilitates their communication at work.

# Coaching by educating

We turn now to what people are more likely to think of as actual *coaching* communication at work -- namely educating those for whom you have supervisory responsibility about communication at work. In a recent book entitled ***The Work of Nations***, Robert B. Reich, 1991, delineates four basic skills which are required of successful, productive 21st Century workers whose workplace is the world economy: *abstraction, system thinking, experimentation* and *collaboration*. The workers who have acquired these skills -- either through formal education and/or on the job -- are called *symbolic analysts* and are the only workers whose future is very promising, according to Reich:

> "Regardless of how your job is officially classi-fied (manufacturing, service, managerial, tech-nical, secretarial, and so on), or the industry in which you work (automotive, steel, computer, advertising, finance, food processing), your real competitive position in the world econ-omy is coming to depend on the function you perform in it. Herein lies the basic reason why incomes are diverging. The fortunes of routine producers are declining. In-person servers are

also becoming poorer, although their fates are less clear-cut. But symbolic analysts -- who solve, identify, and broker new problems -- are, by and large, succeeding in the world economy." p. 208

Whether or not you share Reich's political perspective or his passion for a "positive economic nationalism . . . whose . . . overarching goal is to enhance global welfare rather than to advance one nation's well-being by reducing another's" p. 312 . . . his naming *collaborative team work* as one of four core competencies required of successful new economy workers must be recognized. We agree that, especially in the new economy with the name of the game having changed profoundly, collaborative team work is as important as technical know-how. The next chapter will present what we claim are the necessary and sufficient communication skills for collaborative team work. To be clear about the scope of this claim:

> **The three NEM2 MasterSkills® take the guesswork out of working with people. Competence using the three NEM2 MasterSkills® enables you to cope effectively with any and all interpersonal situations you could confront in the workplace.**

In the face of such a claim, it is no surprise that coaching communication at work by *educating* will be directed toward the **NEM2 MasterSkills®**. We begin by reviewing what most readers know -- the difference between *training* and *educating.* We must acknowledge some impatience in the past with speakers and writers who made a big deal out of the difference -- but who were not able to do either one very effectively. Over the past several years we have observed a very disturbing example of the damage caused by not understanding the difference between *educating and training.*

You could probably guess that one of the three **NEM2 MasterSkills**® for which we claim so much importance in communicating at work is a *listening* skill. You may also know that there are a variety of names for an active listening process -- reflecting, summarizing, etc. We use the name ***paraphrasing*** to refer to the behavior we believe is most effective in communicating to another person that you are listening.

There have been hundreds and hundreds of people who have been put through training on how to be better listeners who have been taught to preface their paraphrases with, "What I hear you saying is. . .". The purpose of training people to use that phrase was to give them an easy way to get started on an unfamiliar response pattern -- namely to acknowledge the speaker and to get clear on what the person really meant before taking issue or arguing with, or redirecting or questioning or ignoring what the person said. No doubt trainers thought they were helping people become better able to communicate.

The actual effect of training people to use, "What I hear you saying is. . ." was two-fold. People who were less skilled at processing the non-verbal cues about the impact they were having on those who had to listen to this robotic, phony, contrived introduction to their para-phrases were seen as manipulative or stupid. People who were more skilled at processing information about their impact could see the destructive effect of introducing "What I hear you saying. . ." into the conversation more than once during an exchange -- they simply stopped paraphrasing. That which was designed to facilitate communication at work actively blocked it from happening.

To educate means *to lead out.* To coach communication at work by *educating* means that the results of your coaching efforts are that the persons you coach are freer -- more able to be clear with others about their ideas, perceptions, concerns, purposes, beliefs and values and to understand the meanings in the ideas, perceptions, concerns, purposes, beliefs and values expressed by others.

There are no quick little phrases you can memorize that will make effective communication at work a cinch. There is a place for drill and practice and training in this skill building arena the way there is with any other skill building effort. However, it is essential that proper respect be given not only to the complexity of **content** people intend to communicate at work but, even more, to the complexity inherent in the **process** of humans communicating with one another at work.

> Simply: all communication skill *training* for the workplace must have educational value or it runs a very high risk of becoming destructive to the well-trained person who mindlessly employees it.

# Coaching by empowerment

It is no longer necessary to persuade readers that organizations -- large and small, public and private, for profit and not for profit -- should benefit from the thinking and ideas of stakeholders at all levels. Facilitating such participation on the part of all workers is understood to be the responsibility of managers/supervisors.

There are two ways that managers/supervisors can empower the workers for whom they have responsibility: 1) facilitate system change and 2) facilitate worker change. Beginning with Peter Block's **The Empowered Manager**, 1987, there have been many very fine offerings directed toward managers/supervisors becoming empowering leaders. Most of the effort -- books, articles and training seminars -- has been focused on the way managers/supervisors can change both the structure and function of the current workplace systems -- #1 above. There has been little written about how to facilitate worker change -- #2 above -- other than through the inspiration that derives from exposing them to the organization's vision.

Nothing could be clearer in the last 5-10 years than the need for organizations to change both their structures and their functioning. We believe, however, that in the rush to make those needed changes, overlooked was the debilitating absence of the fundamental communication skills required to implement TQM/CQI, to reach the **Age of Unreason**, *1989*, to enjoy **Thriving on Chaos**, *1987*, to achieve **Quality Without Tears**, *1984*, to practice the **Fifth Discipline**, *1990*, to become **Peak Performers**, *1986*, to **Driving Fear Out of the Workplace**, *1991*, to **Manage on the Edge**, *1990*, to accept that **Leadership is an Art**, *1989*, as well as appreciate **Leadership Jazz**, *1992*.

We have worked with a model -- which by today's standards is ancient history but -- which has proven very helpful in making the point that to understand the occurrence or non-occurrence of any event, both personal and situational factors must be considered. Fritz Heider in his pivotal work entitled ***The Psychology of Interpersonal Relations***, 1958, presented what he called the *Naive Analysis of Action*: a systematic, common-sense formulation of internal and external factors combining to produce a particular action. The following diagram is a schematic representation of Heider's formulation:

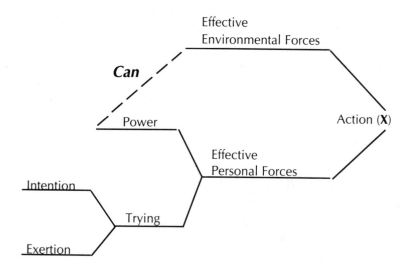

Any Action (**X**) is the result of the Effective Forces of the Person in combination (additive) with the Effective Forces of the Environment. The Effective Forces of the Person are understood to be the Person's Power (abilities, skills, temperament) in combination (multiplicative) with Trying (motivation); the latter being a combination of Intention --what a person is trying to do -- and Exertion -- how hard the person is trying to do it. The Effective Environmental Forces either hinder or facilitate the Personal Forces. The Effective Environmental Forces in combination with the Person's Power determine whether or not the Person **Can** do (**X**), regardless of the Person's Trying. The two conditions of action are **Can** and Trying; that is (**X**) is a function of **Can** (Power and EEF) in combination with Trying (Intention + Exertion).

Using Heider's formulation, *empowerment in the workplace* must be understood in terms of **Can**. Whether or not individuals or a team **Can** carry out particular actions will depend on the Effective Environmental Forces which facilitate or hinder those Actions and the Personal Power individuals or teams are able to direct toward the Actions.

It is true that an organization could be doing everything possible to facilitate participation on the part of individuals and teams at the same time that the teams and individuals possess the necessary Power -- but are just not Trying -- which is why there is no Action. It is possible -- but very unlikely!

It is also true that individuals and teams could possess the necessary skills to accomplish particular Actions *(X)* and also be Trying with all the Intention and Exertion they can muster, but the organization controlling their Effective Environmental Forces hinder those individuals and/or teams to the point that they **Cannot** make **X** happen. It is possible -- but very unlikely!

The reason individuals and teams fail to participate -- fail to take Action -- is rarely because they are not Trying. But neither is it because the organization -- i.e., Effective Environmental Forces -- is blocking the individual's or team's efforts. The primary reason that individuals and teams are not successfully empowered is because they do not have sufficient Personal Power -- they are not *able* to effectively communicate. The ability to communicate effectively in the workplace is absolutely necessary for workers to become empowered in the workplace.

Our contention is that most managers/supervisors do not believe that the problem is a lack of Power (insufficient communication skills) and they keep trying to find other way to inspire their workers and other ways to change their system.

We recommend that managers/supervisors coach communication at work by literally empowering the workers for whom they have responsibility. **Coaching by empowering** the workers then becomes a matter of overseeing a training program from which no one can emerge without having the core competencies required to collaborate in the workplace. We, of course, believe that the **NEM2 MasterSkills**® which will be presented next -- in Chapter 5 -- are the necessary and sufficient core communication competencies for workers to become empowered in the workplace.

Managers/supervisors **who know how to empower** their supervisees through coaching them, actively look for opportunities to engage the people they serve by:

seeking them out

soliciting their thoughts and opinions

listening to them; teaching them to listen

challenging them and encouraging them

connecting them to appropriate resources

offering information and clarification about the organization's *big picture*

telling them stories about the organization

providing clear directives and boundaries -- when and where appropriate

providing direct behavioral feedback about their job performance

engaging them in continuous learning

providing a safe place to practice, stumble, try again and improve

# Communication at Work

# Chapter 5

# NEM2 MasterSkills® for
## *communication at work*

There are three core competencies -- we call them the **NEM2 MasterSkills®** -- that are required of all people who have to collaborate in the workplace. In view of the ways the workplace is changing, that means all people need these three core competencies for communication at work. The three **NEM2 MasterSkills®** are:

***paraphrasing -- performance imaging -- purpose stating***

The theoretical framework and foundation for the **NEM2 MasterSkills®** have been presented in a paper entitled *Focus on Function in an Uncertain World.* Here we will present a very brief summary of that material.

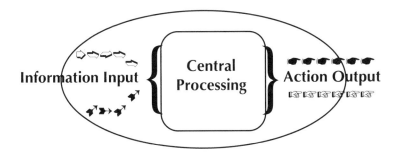

Neither a person nor an organization can count on information from the outside world being absolutely accurate. This is especially true when the information comes from other humans and is about other humans.

Neither a person nor an organization can count on any effort to have impact on the outside world -- action output -- as being 100% successful in achieving the intended purpose. Again, this is especially true when the actions depend on humans and the intended impact is directed toward humans.

We live in a probabilistic world of approximations, guesses, hypotheses and best efforts. Nothing is *absolutely for sure*, there really is no *once and for all* and the **Exact and Very Strange Truth** is -- *nothing ever stays the same*. Therefore, while it is important that we learn as much as possible about our world -- especially about the humans that dominate it -- it is more important to learn to cope with the uncertainty that characterizes human existence. We will not be able to learn enough to render human behavior predictable and controllable in the near future -- if ever. The workplace provides a perfect example of a place where we need to effectively cope with uncertainty -- better known now as *chaos*.

The three **NEM2 MasterSkills®** are used together for communication at work -- they are practically inseparable. But each one has special strength:

> *paraphrasing* for information input
> *performance imaging* for central processing
> *purpose stating* for action output

# Paraphrasing

Whenever you are listening to someone, the ideas the person is communicating could suggest a series of pictures that would illustrate the person's comments. This is, of course, a bit more difficult if the person is giving you highly technical information which could be thought of as a set of very specific instructions. If you were listening to a story that has a beginning and an ending, characters, a setting and a story line, then it is especially easy to *see* a series of images that could tell that story. You might think of this as a *slide show inside your head* illustrating the narration. Even in the case of a person instructing you on how to do something or how to get somewhere, you could *make a movie* or *develop a slide show* inside your head as a way of listening to and understanding what you are being told.

*Paraphrasing* is a brief description, using your own words, of the movie inside your head depicting the speaker's story. The star of the movie inside your head is the speaker. Even if the speaker is talking about someone else, it is still the speaker's reactions -- thoughts and feelings -- about that someone else that you focus on and *paraphrase*.

For example, imagine that your supervisor is telling you about his/her earliest experiences as a line worker before moving into management. Imagine that the supervisor is talking specifically about how difficult his/her boss was. You first make it clear that you are interested in and appreciate the reminiscing. You then demonstrate your interest and appreciation by paraphrasing. Examples of good *paraphrasing*, poor *paraphrasing* and parroting are illustrated in the two examples that follow.

**101**

**You:** I'm really enjoying hearing you talk about your early work experiences.

**Supervisor:** Well, things were different then -- grievance procedures were unheard of. People felt so lucky to have a job they would not have dared to complain . . . that supervisor got away with cruelties you wouldn't believe!

**Good *paraphrase* You:** You've seen lots of changes, including becoming less willing to put up with unreasonable, inhumane treatment from supervisors . . .

**Poor *pararphrase* You:** You like things better now...

**Good *paraphrase* You:** You would find yourself just absorbing stuff from the supervisor because neither you -- nor anyone else -- knew any better.

**Parroting You:** It's hard to believe how supervisors got away with being so cruel . . . .

Take another example: Imagine you and a co-worker are discussing how your efforts to try to understand your co-worker were received by the co-worker. After making your purposes clear, you receive your co-worker's comments by ***paraphrasing*** them.

|          | **You:** | Mark, I would like to ask a favor . . . . It would be helpful to me if you would tell me how you felt when I stepped into the conversation this morning in the staff meeting -- you know, when you were talking to Dave. |
|----------|----------|---|
|          | **Mark:** | Oh yeah . . . yeah, well that was fine. |
| *Paraphrase* | **You:** | What I did was O.K. with you. |
|          | **Mark:** | Yeah, well I don't think he understood what I was tryin' to say and then what you said made him see it. |
| *Paraphrase* | **You:** | It clarified it -- what I said clarified . . . |
|          | **Mark:** | Yeah -- I think he was gettin' pretty mad before you said what you did. . . . but then he seemed to calm down some. |

It is not possible to exaggerate the importance to you of developing your ***paraphrasing*** skills. We believe that more communication errors result from the absence or inadequacy of **paraphrasing** than from any other single cause.

This multi-purpose communication tool can be used in many ways to accomplish a number of interpersonal tasks:

1 **Assist you listen carefully**. If you expect to accurately reflect the images which have been shared with you, then you must attend carefully, visualize the images and describe them.

2 **Affirm that you care** enough about the speaker to listen carefully. If people cannot tell what your response to their comment is, they will circle back, repeat, pause expectantly, etc., in order to get an indication that at least you hear them and hopefully understand them -- although you may disagree with them.

3 **Afford an opportunity for the speaker to correct you** if you are getting off track. It is disappointing on both sides of a conversation to discover that the speaker *lost* the listener way back somewhere and the listener has been confused and/or tuned out ever since. The pain and frustration of not understanding and not being understood can be avoided through frequent brief *paraphrasing*.

4 **Allow the speaker to edit and clarify**. Sometimes the speaker does not say what s/he means to say. Upon hearing her/his comments reflected in a **paraphrase** -- even one that is not perfectly accurate -- the speaker can revise, clarify, modify what was said originally.

5 **Allow the speaker to lead you** through a personal experience or set of feelings which the speaker wants to
share with you. Even when the speaker wants very
much to share thoughts and feelings and even though
you, the listener, are committed to intensive listening,
unless you *paraphrase* the shared journey will bog
down or end prematurely.

6 **Avoid unnecessary hassles**, arguments and debates.
Discussion and decision making can proceed more
constructively as each person listens carefully and ac-
knowledges the other through *paraphrasing*, before
asserting her/his own position.

**The defining characteristics of a good *paraphrase*:**

- it is brief
  - it is pictorial
    - it contains both facts and feelings
      - it is focused on the speaker's experience

It is also possible to identify what should be avoided in
attempting to *paraphrase*. A *paraphrase* should not:

- be insincere -- faked interest in the speaker

- be judgmental -- packaged with your own feelings
  about what the speaker shared

- be a request for specific new information

(continuing, **a paraphrase should not:**)

- **be an interpretation -- it should not go beyond what the speaker has shared**

- **be a subtle leading of the speaker**

- **be an example from your own life**

- **be much more or much less intense than what the speaker was feeling**

- **be initiated with, "What I hear you saying is . . . " nor any other statement that begins with "I. . ."**

Before we proceed to the next **NEM2 MasterSkill®**, namely *performance imaging*, we want to make a distinction between *paraphrasing* and something that people have been erroneously taught is *paraphrasing*.

A listening skill that belongs in pastoral or clinical settings or in the privacy and intimacy of the home, namely *perception checking*, has been presented in the workplace as an ordinary listening skill.

There are times when you will experience yourself as having *perceived* another person's attitude or emotional state or motive, even though the person does not say anything directly. If you were to check the accuracy of your *perception* by inquiring of the person, you would be using *perception checking* to confirm or disconfirm your inference/hunch.

Even though you see things in people regularly that are defensive or distorted, you need not feel compelled to pounce on it, shine bright lights on it and reveal the hidden truth. With the following examples, you can see why we caution people so strongly about the use and misuse of *perception checking.*

## Example #1

**Co-worker:** Frankly, I don't really care which part I do . . . . just so it gets done! . . . .

**You:** I just need to check something out . . . . I've known you for six years and the only other time I've seen you look and act this way was when your daughter was so very sick . . . . I know you haven't said anything and maybe I'm not the one to talk with, but I can't just ignore it!

**Co-worker:** I can't talk . . . I probably should, but . . . it's stuff at home and work too . . . I really appreciate your concern . . . maybe in a few days we could talk after work . . . . I just need to hang on right now . . . . Thanks.

When you *look beyond* what someone has said, when you *see behind* or *see through* the defenses by means of which a person is coping, you may take away something that the person needs. Ripping away people's defenses, because you are discerning enough to do so, is wrong.

**Example #2**

> **You:** I need this information before 10:00 o'clock when the site team will be in our department.
>
> **Co-worker:** You look really tired and upset. Is something really bothering you?
>
> **You:** I don't know what you mean . . . .I guess I always look this way at 8:00 a.m. . . . I don't know of anything special that's bothering me . . . . except this whole project may be dumped . . . . but I sure don't want to talk about it now or with you!

The purposes of perception checking are:

1  to reveal some acknowledged, hidden meaning, feeling, attitude or motive

2  to move very close to another person by letting her/him know how thoroughly you understand her/him

3  to up-end, throw off balance or disorient someone and thereby gain control of the situation

*Perception checking* -- speculating and inquiring about people beyond what they voluntarily reveal -- is a very valuable communication tool in the right hands being used for appropriate purposes.

Misuses or abuses of *perception checking* are most likely to occur when someone in power -- without any clear purpose for demanding the information -- asks about unacknowledged feelings within someone who has less power. This is especially dangerous when the power person has no awareness of nor any regard for the possible importance of the person keeping the material hidden.

Our primary purpose here is to warn you, the reader, against substituting a *perception check* for a **paraphrase.** They are very different and mixing them may surprise you with an unanticipated explosion. The occasions when you would legitimately need to use *perception checking* in the workplace are few and far between.

# Performance Imaging

**Performance imaging,** the second **NEM2 MasterSkills®,** has been referred to by a variety of names: *mental rehearsal, visualization, guided fantasy, meditation, neurolinguistic programming,* etc. Each of these human processes makes use of: **Attending** -- focusing -- which is combined with **Imaging** -- visual, auditory, tactile, somatic -- and, usually, further combined with **Relaxing** to achieve heightened awareness. You may want to note the acronym **AIR --** there are several ways in which it is quite apt.

**Attending --** to stretch to; to direct the mind or energies to, to turn one's ear to, to regard, consider, wait for, expect.
**Imaging --** to represent, portray, delineate, reflect, represent to oneself, symbolize, devise, plan.
**Relaxing --** to make less dense, less restricted, less rigid, less severe, less stiff; to release, to free.

Your being able to learn *performance imaging* depends on your *AIR* supply. As you know, even though you cannot point to it or take a picture of it, your air supply is essential for your well-being. So too is the *performance imaging* process going on within you -- which you can neither point to nor photograph. However, just as is true in the case of your air supply, if your *attending, imaging* and *relaxing* are disturbed, then your ability to perform will also be limited.

*Performance Imaging:*

• takes place within you -- privately

• happens within you many times each day

• resembles -- but is different from -- remembering or thinking

• is a natural process you can learn to develop

• is easier for some people than it is for others

We will now very briefly examine these three aspects of *performance imaging* -- not because with such insight a person could master this very important communication tool. The only way a person can learn to be more skillful with **performance imaging**, is to practice, practice and practice. However, if you are convinced that this second **NEM2 MasterSkill**® is extremely important for communication at work, then you might pursue learning experiences characterized as *practice with coaching -- such as a learning transfer team with a coach/facilitator.*

**Attending** can easily be illustrated by asking you to freeze in position right now -- that is, do not move for a few moments. Audit your body -- head-to-toe, without shifting or moving, tune into how each part of your body is feeling. Almost invariably, what people find is that some part of their body is uncomfortable -- maybe even in pain -- and now that they are **attending** to it, they certainly would adjust the uncomfortable part. Stop for a moment and listen to all the noises around you that you are not **attending** to, while you read. Finally, all of us have had the very defeating experience of trying consciously to **not attend** to something. **Unless you intentionally attend to something else, you cannot *not* attend to something.**

**Imaging** can appear through several channels. Imaging also needs to be distinguished from remembering and thinking. Remember the last time you changed a flat tire or entered a house where bread was baking or shook hands with someone.

- **imagine the sound of lug nuts hitting the hubcap**

- **imagine the smell of baking bread**

- **imagine the feeling of extending, clasping and releasing**

Even if you are not able to remember changing a tire or entering where bread is baking or shaking hands, you can *imagine* each one.

We all use **imaging** regularly.  Picture a time when you had to repair or replace something that you could feel but not see. . . had to reach into or around and screw or unscrew, plug or unplug. . .somehow your fingers could 'see'.  Think about your hands knowing where the light switch is in a dark room.  Think about steering a car without thinking about it!  Imagine the sound of a car crashing into another car -- you *hear* it and, of course, you do not *hear* it.

Finally, for those who do not already know how to **relax** deeply by simply instructing yourself to "relax" we encourage you learn to relax.  For example, where ever you are sitting now, get yourself into a reasonably comfortable, secure feeling position and begin to focus on your breathing.  Just quietly to yourself, with your eyes closed, count your breathing -- count "one" for in and "two" for out, "one" for in "two" for out over and over.  Most people, almost immediately upon getting focused, will begin to breathe more slowly and more deeply without any conscious effort to do so.

All human activity has the potential for reaching higher levels of excellence, when the people taking action are in charge of how tense or relaxed they are.  Fortunately there are many inexpensive, relatively painless ways to learn to relax.  There have also been applications of **relaxation** to a range of human performance arenas.  Please refer to:

***Beyond the Relaxation Response***, 1984
***Focusing***, 1978.

*The Relaxation and Stress Reduction Workbook*, 1988.
*Sporting Body Sporting Mind*, 1984.
*A Soprano on Her Head*, 1982.
*Take a Deep Breath*, 1986.

Examples of *performance imaging* that require **AIR --** **attending**/ focusing combined with **imaging** -- and that combination blended with **relaxing**:

> 40 yard touch down pass
> chipping in from 50 yards
> splitting wood for an hour
> having a voice left in the Third Act
> installing a cardiac pacemaker
> dress rehearsals
> child birth classes
> pre-shot routines

Unfortunately, we also use *performance imaging* in a self-sabotage manner. For example, when we ruminate about a problem -- "I can't even imagine what will happen. . .I don't know what to do!" Worse yet, we sometimes re-hearse disaster -- "Oh, I can just see how awful it will be. . .I know I'll make a fool of myself!" These are both examples of the destructive use of *performance imaging*.

The *good news* is that with **practice**, you can greatly improve your *performance imaging* skills. If you actively, intentionally use *performance imaging* to enhance your perceiving, thinking and acting -- you will greatly improve your communication at work performance. We suggest that you review Chapter 3, the discussions of barriers blocking communication at work. It is easy to appreciate how much the **NEM2 MasterSkill®** *performance imaging* can help remove those barriers.

## Purpose Stating

Communication at work becomes optimally collaborative and constructive when discussions, debates and decision-making are characterized by a spirit of open inquiry. Particularly, if you occupy a position of power -- boss/supervisor -- but even if power is attributed to you because of your *presence* and/or verbal fluency, you should help project a spirit of open inquiry, namely:

- eagerness to perceive and understand,
- intentional avoidance of prejudging,
- respectfulness for people disclosing their personal facts and feelings,
- honestly admitting if and when you are confused
- willingness to work hard to gain full understanding of the issue and options.

If you become skillful establishing and modeling such a spirit of open inquiry, others will very likely join you. It is quite natural for humans, even if they are adversaries in contention, to be motivated to find a fair resolution to their concerns -- **especially if they do not feel an immediate need to protect or defend themselves.**

If the process is begun early enough, the task will be to encourage the cooperative problem-solving that is so natural for groups of humans and to discourage or eliminate the hostile retaliatory actions that are also natural for people in groups.

**Humans are naturally:**

- **curious and active**

- **interested in new, novel, unfamiliar experiences**

- **learning most of the time**

- **motivated by opportunities to understand things, information and people**

- **motivated by opportunities to have impact on things, information and people**

However, humans must learn to protect and defend themselves from things, information and/or people that threaten their well being. When humans are protecting and defending, they are no longer active, curious, open to new experience. When humans are protecting and defending themselves, they are reduced to attacking or hiding.

If you are a manager/supervisor, you must learn how to avoid being experienced as threatening to people. They will, in turn, be more likely to remain active and open; they will not need to hide from you or attack you. The **NEM2 MasterSkill®** *purpose stating* is the most effective way for a potentially threatening person to make inquiry without making people defensive.

The first step toward becoming a trustworthy, approachable person with whom others can consult and cooperate, but need not defend against, is **to make your purposes clear**. Your taking this first step tends to call the same behavior from others. Not only do you need to make your purposes clear and invite others to make their purposes clear at the outset of most interactions/meetings, but you will also need to reiterate your purposes and request a restatement of others' purposes throughout interactions/meetings that go on for extended periods of time.

Examples of *openers* for **purpose statements** include:

"My purpose is to. . ."
"I am trying to. . . "
"I have three objectives. . . "
"I am pushing for. . . "
"I intend to. . . "
"The direction I want this to go is. . ."
"I want you to....so I can. . . "
"What I'm trying to make happen is. . . "
"I would like to see us. . .
"It would be helpful to me. . ."
"My role and responsibilities demand that. . ."
"My goal for. . .is. . ."
"I am rapidly moving toward. . ."

Typically people assume that others somehow know what their purposes are; they may even feel silly stating what they assume is obvious. **Rarely is it obvious to one person exactly what another one is intending**.

It is understandable why the absence of a clear purpose statement is upsetting. People automatically guard against what they do not understand. Not making purposes clear could mean a ruthless, vicious attack might be unleashed without warning. Not making purposes clear could also mean that passive aggressive blocking and thwarting would undermine attempts to collaborate. Not making purposes clear might not signal anything sinister, but in the absence of a clear understanding of purpose, people become defensive.

Constructive communication requires that you be clear about what it is you are trying to accomplish; an accurate statement of purpose is the necessary skill. ***Purpose stating*** is one of the three **NEM2 MasterSkills®.**

Strangely enough, the route most people take instead of making a ***purpose statement***, is to ask a question. Most people consider asking questions to be an innocent, non-intrusive, non-aggressive way of approaching another person. Asking questions is certainly not something that you need to worry might make people defensive! However, ask yourself, "do I like to be questioned?"

Walk through the following set of questions and answers; hopefully it will be clear that the opportunity for people to become defensive about being questioned is greater than the chances they will merely be open to inquiry.

Why do people ask questions? Why do **you** ask questions?

Why do we ask about the purpose of your questions?

How important is all this questioning of questioning?

**117**

# Communication at Work

Question #1: Why do people ask questions?

Answer #1: There are many reasons why people ask questions; common reasons are:

1 to obtain information; to find something

2 to be friendly, cordial, sociable

3 to suggest, indirectly, an idea or thought

4 to stimulate thinking about a topic

5 to intimidate the one being interrogated

6 to impugn the target of inquisition

7 to insult the target of interrogation

8 to indirectly accuse the one questioned

9 to totally control the verbal interaction

10 to avoid disclosing one's own position while continuing to uncover another's

Question #2: Why do **you** ask questions?

Answer #2: Only **you** could answer why it is you ask questions -- each time you ask one; it's a very personal matter.

Question #3:    Why do we ask you about the purpose
                of your questions?

Answer #3:      We ask about the purposes of your
                questioning to stimulate your thinking.

Question #4:    How important is all this questioning of
                questioning?

Answer #4:      The difference between being ques-
                tioned for any of the first four purposes
                identified above and any of the remain
                six is the difference between experienc-
                ing benevolence and malevolence --
                the difference between feeling some-
                thing good vs. something evil is ap-
                proaching you.

Large numbers of people in the workplace, especially
managers/supervisors, spend much of their work day
gathering and using information from other people. To
secure the information -- which does not always appear as
planned or on time -- inquiry must be made of a variety of
others: co-workers, superiors, customers, vendors, team
members, adversaries, subordinates and stakeholders.

When question asking is used to make inquiry, the person
being questioned is more often than not unclear as to what
the purpose of the questioning actually is. Without a clear
signal that one of the first four purposes listed above
prompts the question, the remaining six purposes are believable candidates for explaining:  "Why am I being
questioned?"  The traditional authority associated with
managers/supervisors makes their questioning especially
threatening.

Consider for a moment the connotations of these words which refer to asking questions:

> inquisition
>> interrogation
>>> investigating
>>>> questioning
>>>>> quizzing

These words do not call up images of people sharing an open spirit of inquiry while engaged in productive discussions. Instead, they suggest a process intended to test, to trap, to reveal wrongdoing and to condemn. In contrast, stating clearly what your purposes are, providing a context for your inquiry and specifying what you intend to do with any information you receive has a better chance of opening an honest inquiry.

Ideally, *questioning* in western cultures would be an invitation to join with the questioner in a process of inquiry during which you would together discover and develop ways to improve upon the present for the future. Unfortunately, *questioning* in western cultures is more often a backward focused evaluation of how well or poorly a person has done.

"Now what have you done?" and "Why did you do that?", are two dreadful questions that Anglo-European children have hurled at them hundreds and hundreds of times before they leave their teens. What these children soon learn and carry into adulthood is that these *so-called* questions are more indictments than genuine questions and no one is truly interested in listening to their answers. It is rare in the life of an occidental young person that being questioned is an invitation to think together and work together. Unfortunately, the majority conclude that people in authority do not value their thinking and are rarely, if ever, interested in what they have to say.

These people then enter a workplace and are expected to know how to and be willing to engage actively in team work, participation and joint problem-solving. The supervisors of these folks -- trying to facilitate participation and engage workers in CQI -- have been encouraged to ask an unending number of questions of them. It is probably not good advice for drawing out Occidentals.

You may regard yourself as an especially good interviewer/conversationalist -- a person who knows how to ask really interesting questions. You may be regarded as a very astute fact finder -- a person who knows how to ask penetrating questions that get to the heart of the matter. You may have read books, listened to tapes or attended workshops wherein you learned probing and open-ended questioning techniques. You may have trouble believing that what you regard as asking an innocent question merely to gather a small piece of information could be experienced as *questioning* another.

You may believe that you do not mind being *questioned* and even welcome the opportunity to share ideas. However, without a description of the context within which a question is being asked, the purpose of the question and the use to which the answer will be put, most Occidentals will experience themselves as *on the spot* when being *questioned* and they do not like it.

**Effective supervision, as well as team building, collaborative problem solving and contention management all require that people keep track of their purposes and communicate those purposes to others.**

The major block to such constructive communication is not that people are unwilling to be clear about their purposes. The major block is that people are **unskilled** in clarifying their purposes and speaking to others about them as the first steps in accomplishing them.

Therefore, if you want to increase your competence in communicating a genuine spirit of open inquiry and successfully engaging others in a process of open and honest inquiry, then you will learn how to reframe questions into *purpose statements*.

The **NEM2 MasterSkill®** *purpose stating* is the most effective way to reduce the amount of *questioning* you use. We are not interested in removing any tools from your communication tool box; we are interested in your adding tools that increase the range of people, places and problems you can engage in a spirit of open inquiry. Since asking questions is an extremely well-rehearsed form of conversing for most people, it is not easy to master another format. We encourage you to do whatever it takes, however, to learn *purpose stating.*

In the past -- *Communication at Work,* 2nd Edition -- we discussed another communication tool which is worthy of mention here, *preference stating,* but does not have the stature of the **NEM2 MasterSkill®** *purpose stating.* Preference stating can be very useful to well-functioning teams or to newly formed teams trying to work together skillfully. We would caution that *preference stating* can never be an effective substitute for *purpose stating.* If purposes have been made clear, then knowing team members' preferences can be helpful. Examples of *openers* for *preference stating* follow:

- "If I had only myself to think about, I would. . ."

- "If it were up to me and everyone were automatically pleased with what I said, I would. . ."

- "My preference is slight and what you want probably means more to me than what I want. . ."

- "What would really please me would be to know you were pleased. . ."

- "I would like you to decide. . ."

- "I wish I could tell you what I want, but I can only say what I don't want. . ."

There are considerable individual differences in how complex and how intense people's preferences are. For example, ask yourself or think about asking the people with whom you work to make a list of things that could be enjoyed together. Some people can identify a dozen different things they would enjoy doing; others would have trouble identifying anything they would like to do with others in the office. For some people, feeling mildly positive about an activity warrants describing that activity as something they enjoy or like. "I like", for others requires feeling **very** strongly about it. Therefore, some people cannot name things they would enjoy doing with their co-workers because they would have to be ecstatic about an activity before they would name it as a preference and they are not ecstatic about anything involving co-workers.

Some other people cannot generate a list of preferred activities because they think in terms of what they do **not** like and what is least preferred and, thus, to be avoided. If you ask them what they prefer or would like to do, they are blank, but they can veto with energy and conviction.

People in both instances -- people who require ecstasy in order to label something a preference and people who only know what they do **not** like -- have some difficulty experiencing, much less reporting on, their likes and their preferences.

There are also a fair number of people who have well defined and sometimes very strong preferences, but who are often unaware of these preferences. They may say: "I don't care," or, "Whatever is O.K. with you," or, "Whatever you would like," when in fact, they do care. Any number of possibilities would *not* be O.K. and "Whatever you would like," would be fine -- as long as you like the right things. This is, sadly, a very common pattern and most of us, when told, "Oh, I don't care. . .whatever you would like", are disbelieving.

Typically you would say, "Are you sure?" Most of us have had the experience of being told that a person has no particular preference and then found out later this co-worker really preferred things to be different. Often times, there would have been no problem arranging things so that both you and the co-worker could have had what you both preferred -- except, without the information you cannot arrange things to suit both of you. Once again, the absence of information blocks people from doing excellent problem solving.

It is true, whenever you disclose your preferences, it increases your vulnerability because people are in a position to deny/reject you. It is also true that once having made clear what you would prefer, it is possible for people to act accordingly even when they are not sincere. You cannot be certain that a person does not feel coerced by your clear *preference statement*. Whereas, if you are vague and they guess correctly, it somehow reassures most of us that the person is sincere.

*Preference statements* facilitate constructive communication because they clarify and suggest possibilities, but individuals who make clear *preference statements* are more vulnerable than are people who do not let anyone know what they prefer and prize. However, if people are forthright and disclosing by **stating their purposes**, then the vulnerability of *stating preferences* is negligible.

## NEM2 MasterSkills® are practically inseparable

If you put effort into becoming a very fine listener through the **NEM2 MasterSkill®** *paraphrasing* and if you put effort into becoming a constructive team member by routinely and repeatedly using **NEM2 MasterSkill®** *purpose stating* both for yourself and others and if you take responsibility for your impact through the **NEM2 MasterSkill®** *performance imaging*, you will be a very effective communicator at work.

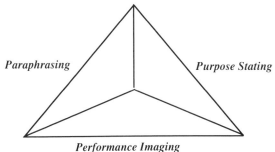

*Paraphrasing*     *Purpose Stating*

*Performance Imaging*

The three **NEM2 MasterSkills®** *paraphrasing, purpose stating* and *performance imaging* are all you need to accomplish what was stated as the purpose of this book -

becoming an effective communicator at work. Of course, there is not an exact formula for the ideal frequency and sequence of **NEM2 MasterSkills**® use in workplace transactions. When they are used effectively, the **NEM2 MasterSkills**® do not stand out -- they are unobtrusive, but not hidden.

When the three **NEM2 MasterSkills**®, taken together, are used within one of three distinct time perspectives -- namely *past, present* and *future* -- three distinct **Master-Strategies**® emerge.

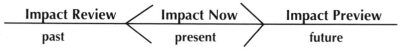

| Impact Review | Impact Now | Impact Preview |
|:---:|:---:|:---:|
| past | present | future |

When you direct your attention to events of the past, you know you cannot change that which is locked in history but hopefully -- you can learn something which will inform the future. When you direct the three **NEM2 MasterSkills**® toward the *past* in order to learn from experience that is called an ***Impact Review***.

When you direct your attention to events that will be happening in the future, you know you cannot absolutely dictate what will take place but hopefully -- you can shape the future through planning and preparation. Directing the three **NEM2 MasterSkills**® toward the future is called an ***Impact Preview***.

When you use the three **NEM2 MasterSkills**® to regulate your own behavior by monitoring real time events -- of which you are a part -- that is called ***Impact Now***. Because of the speed with which information is moving, ***Impact Now*** is significantly more difficult to master than ***Impact Preview*** or ***Impact Review***.

# NEM2 MasterStrategy®:  Impact Preview

- **Imagine the situation you expect to encounter**

- **Clarify your purposes -- all of them**

- **Commit yourself to having a positive impact**

- **Picture an ideal process and outcome**

- **Picture the worst and yourself handling it effectively**

- **Identify information/skills you need to be effective**

- **Picture being effective -- no matter how bad it gets**

- **Encourage yourself -- celebrate a job well done**

*Impact Preview* is a process of using ***performance imaging*** to focus on a situation you will be encountering, inquiring of yourself what your purposes are, committing yourself to having a positive impact, visualizing the ways you are most likely to produce the positive impact you desire, and in your mind's eye, coaching yourself how to manage yourself step-by-step from beginning to end.

The purpose of taking yourself through an *Impact Preview* is to prepare yourself to effectively handle anything that may arise in a specific upcoming situation.  Obviously, if you have no advance warning that you are going to be confronted with a particular situation, you cannot do an

*Impact Preview.* Looking ahead, anticipating the behavior of others, projecting a picture of your own behavior and planning the impact you would choose to have -- all are proactive self-management procedures which characterize *Impact Preview.*

When you say to yourself, "Imagine the situation you will be encountering", you should include in the picture both the physical surroundings in vivid detail and the significant other people. For example, suppose you were going to do an *Impact Preview* of a typical Monday morning in your work place. . .

> Begin by picturing how you and others arrive at the work place...in your mind's eye and ear *see* yourself and others entering the work place, *hear* the Monday morning sounds of people and machines -- cars, buses, trucks, elevators, subways, radios, children, police, word processors, medical monitors, drills, earth movers.

> Move forward in time by picturing the passing of each hour in your work place. By emphasizing physical imagery you can begin to understand how various people may be feeling. See people moving about in characteristic ways, vividly imagine the human noises and the machine noises. See yourself in the picture; observe you from your boss' point of view and observe you from a coworker's point of view. See yourself moving about; hear the sound of your voice.

> Now focus on the most significant people in your work world. Understand them in such a way that you will be better able to anticipate their behavior

and not be surprised by the way they handle particular situations. Think of each significant co-
worker in terms of style. Compare that person's
style with your own style in terms of pace, emotionality and purpose. Vividly imagine each co-
worker moving about your work place in her/his
characteristic manner. Move ahead to how the
person leaves the work place, typically. Hear the
sounds, sense the movement, feel the intensity as
various persons end their work that day.

**The first step** -- _imagining the situation you will be
encountering_ -- may involve picturing an office in which
you know every nook and cranny or it might be imagining
a meeting in an office conference room that you have
never seen before. In the first instance, you are recalling
what you know and projecting it; in the second case you
are conjuring up an image which would fit the information you have -- large building, new buildings, downtown
-- and projecting a fantasy. Fortunately the image does not
need to be perfect; it needs to be vivid and real.

**The second step** -- _inquiring of yourself what your
purposes are_ -- could end quickly if, upon asking yourself,
you realize that you do not really care what happens in the
situation, short of a fire or flood; whatever others say or do
is fine, and whatever you say or do is fine with you. This
would be highly unusual because most people entering a
particular work situation do have some investments regarding the direction in which things move, the pace at
which they move, how they are viewed by others in the
situation, and how they view themselves. Think back over
some of the suggestions for **purposes statements**:

What I am trying to make happen . . .
What I am trying to accomplish . . .
The outcome I'm hoping for . . .
My purpose is to . . .
The direction I want this to move . . .

These can serve as leads for specifying your purposes in particular situations. Usually people have more than one purpose and often these purposes seem incompatible. A major stumbling block to constructive communication is *purposes unclear.* Unclear purposes are often the result of a person having what seem to be contradictory purposes, but upon closer view, the purposes are not truly contradictory.

For example, you may want to register a serious objection with a supervisor but also sound a note of cooperation and good will. Or taking another example, you may want to compliment and praise your boss but also avoid giving the appearance of trying to smoothly manipulate your way into a more favorable position. Untangling seemingly contradictory purposes begins with *putting all your cards on the table* -- that is, stating and clarifying each of your purposes. Therefore, in your **Impact Preview**, step two is to state and clarify to yourself each of your purposes in the situation that looms up ahead.

**The third step** -- *committing yourself to having a positive impact* -- becomes a meaningful process, if you have the situation pictured vividly and have clarified your purposes to yourself. There are thoughts and feelings which would interfere with a commitment to be constructive -- for example, terror, revenge and cynicism. If you are immobilized with fear and anxiety, if you are consumed with a desire for revenge, if you are saturated with cynical thoughts and feelings, then the chances of your making a clear commitment to having a positive impact are remote, at best.

You do not have to be swept away on an optimistic cloud of euphoric self-confidence in order to play the role of someone who is committed to having a positive impact. You must know the setting, your purposes, the other characters, opening and closing lines, entrances and exits and above all, you need to be authentically who you are.

The more you develop skill in using **NEM2 MasterSkills®:** *performance imaging, purpose stating* and *paraphrasing,* the less terrified, vindictive and disdainful you will become. Role taking and behavioral rehearsal in the process of acquiring these skills are often the first steps in having a destructive cycle of fear, disdain and revenge become a constructive cycle of understanding, acceptance and affirmation.

"What's the worst thing that can happen?" "Can I survive that?" are two questions which move people forward in committing themselves to positive action. "If I do nothing, things will likely get worse, not better!" is another reminder that mobilizes people to take positive action. "Even if I'm not successful, I will have the satisfaction of having tried!" is another self-statement that promotes positive action. Such **self talk** is a major vehicle for moving forward.

Telling selected other people -- trusted, respected friends and colleagues -- what your purposes and plans are also greatly increases your commitment to positive action. In fact, if you are able to engage in an ***Impact Preview*** in the presence of a supportive colleague, you may find that to be very helpful.

Depending on style, some folks will prefer to do the whole process with someone else. However extensive or limited the involvement of another, telling a respected person that you are going to do "X" with the intention of having a constructive effect, increases your chances of accomplishing it.

If you have removed all barriers blocking your intention to have a positive impact and you are, in fact, committed to having a positive impact, then the next step is to imagine a realistic sequence of interpersonal exchanges. **Performance image** the interaction going very smoothly toward the outcome you seek.

**Performance image** the interaction taking a very negative turn -- imagine the worst! Now figure out what you could do to at least manage yourself with dignity -- even in the face of the worst. Remember to **restate your purposes** and to use **paraphrasing** to give evidence that you have listened.

It is impossible to create a simple, fool-proof formula that will specify what to do and exactly when to do it. You need to be skillful in executing each **NEM2 MasterSkill**®, clear about your purposes and have the courage to keep trying -- to not give up just because it is tough.

**Performance image** yourself **stating your purposes, paraphrasing** and **restating your purposes** in whatever situation you are previewing. You need to be able to imagine vividly how the  situation would appear, how you would appear, how you would sound and how you would feel.

At this point, some people attempt to prepare a script and *block the scenes* so rigidly that they do themselves a great disservice. Obviously, if you develop such a fixed view of what is to come that you are thrown off by anything unanticipated, you would probably be further ahead to do nothing but tell yourself to "just relax and do the best you can".

But an **Impact Preview** does not mean *fasten on a narrow idea of exactly what will happen and do not let go of it no matter what happens.* Instead, it means *consider the full range of possibilities, likely and unlikely; be prepared for things to develop any number of ways; have a clear picture of what you would like to see happen and let that guide your choices.*

We turn now to using the **NEM2 MasterSkills**® to learn from experience by conducting an **Impact Review.**

# NEM2 MasterStrategy®: Impact Review

**Picture telling the story to a respected friend**
- the situation
- your purposes
- the players
- what happened

**Celebrate your positive choices and actions**
- preparing with an *Impact Preview*
- *stating your purposes*
- listening with *paraphrasing*
- monitoring with *Impact Now*

**Confront what needs improvement in your performance**
- review it without ridicule
- review it without ruminating
- review it without rationalizing

**Coach yourself for improved performance**
- image what you could have done better
- clarify what was blocking you
- identify activities that lead to improvement
- encourage yourself

Just as the words suggest, an *Impact Review* is a process of looking back over what is now locked in history, about which nothing can be altered, to recognize and give credit for the positive outcomes that occurred, to face up to the deficits and to plan for and encourage improvement next time.

There are three pitfalls to be avoided in an **Impact Review:**

1 Ridiculing yourself.
2 Ruminating about the past.
3 Rationalizing about actions.

**Do Not Ridicule!** Unfortunately few people learn what it means to pat themselves on the back, celebrate their own right doing, speak to themselves respectfully and appreciatively, take pride in their own successes, give themselves well-deserved praise. On the other hand, most people learn to make fun of themselves, be disrespectful, sarcastic, disgusted with themselves, harshly take themselves to task, blame themselves unreasonably, criticize themselves unmercifully, draw attention to and focus heavily on their faults.

It is with some trepidation that we suggest that you review your performance in a particular situation, evaluate it and celebrate the positive parts. Most people are not very skilled when it comes to celebrating routine, ordinary accomplishments -- especially their own. Encouraging you to do an **Impact Review** may give you license to rip and tear at yourself for your faults and shortcomings, even though it is the opposite effect we are trying to have.

To avoid the pitfall of ridicule during an **Impact Review,** first desensitize yourself to the sound of positive self-references. Make a list of positive statements about yourself -- affirmations -- that you know are true and read them aloud. Tape record your reading. As you replay the audio or video tape of your own voice speaking affirmations, you will see how difficult it is to listen to, accept and appreciate personal affirmations.

An illustrative list of affirmations follows:

- I am eager to learn new things.
- I try hard to improve myself.
- I am sincere about facing my faults.
- I have made progress on becoming more understanding.
- I am learning to be more accepting.
- I encourage others more often.
- I make fewer hostile, unkind remarks.
- I try to do something, rather than just complain.

Once you rid yourself of the tendency to be nasty and harsh with yourself, you can begin to skillfully celebrate your progress without mixed messages.

**Do Not Ruminate!** It is true that no matter how many times it is said that the purpose of reviewing shortcomings is to be optimistically planning for future efforts, some people will interpret *Impact Review* to mean wallow pessimistically in the past. If people review a messy or ugly situation by reliving the disaster -- seeing it, hearing it, feeling it, etc. -- and do no more than that, they are rehearsing doom and gloom. They are practicing future disasters. In contrast, if people review situations, identify the ways their impact could be improved, move toward thinking and planning how to make that improvement, they are rehearsing new, positive possibilities. They are practicing future successes. Some people are such chronic ruminators that they need to learn thought stoppage and self-instruction tactics to manage this tendency during an *Impact Review*.

We have discussed changing the tone and quality of self talk inside your head to be more constructive and more encouraging. We have not discussed the first link in a chain of positive self-references: *thought stoppage.*

Many people need a rather forceful way of putting a stop to all the negative self-references to which they subject themselves before they can begin the chain of positive self-references. Vividly imagine yourself shouting "**STOP!**" and simultaneously seeing the word **STOP!** flashing as a huge red/white neon sign which is signalling "**STOP!**" to whatever unwanted thoughts are filling your head. When people are first learning thought stoppage they are usually encouraged to practice someplace where they really can shout "**STOP!**" at the top of their lungs; they then have a more vivid image of how it sounds.

Once learned, the technique can be used anywhere, of course, because it is all done through your own imagination and visualization. It is also important, especially for beginners, that several positive self-references are ready to go into place immediately following the thought stoppage.

As you learn to master **Impact Review** which is intended to be a proactive and positive self-management strategy, you should be able to reduce the frequency and intensity of your negative self-references.

**Do Not Rationalize!** Humans are naturally curious and have learned from earliest days to ask *"why?"* very frequently. However, when it comes to reviewing their own impact in a situation and explaining *why things developed the way they did*, people undertake an exceedingly complex task. Humans have an interesting tendency to explain the things they have done in such a way that their behavior is consistent with what they believe their values to be. Consistency is important to humans, but some of it is manufactured after the fact.

For example, among co-workers you will sometimes join in the criticism of a superior's incompetence and at another time applaud the same person's competencies. This 180 degree fluctuation in your position may result from something as superficial as the superior having just been friendly in the lunchroom. The superior's competencies do not change and your objective assessment would not be different, but how critical or complimentary about the boss you are among co-workers can vary greatly. If asked, you probably would rationalize your contradictory statements in terms of *having been too harsh before* or *seeing things differently* rather than recognizing that it is much more difficult to be critical and sarcastic about someone with whom you identify personally -- someone who has been cordial to you -- than about the more remote impersonal role, *Boss*.

It is very important for us to see ourselves as in charge of what is happening to us and to think of ourselves as consistent, reasonable folks. Most of us find it unthinkable that our speaking out in a group depends upon such irrelevancies as whether or not we found a parking space easily, whether we were late or on time, how bad traffic was, the status of people in the group, etc. We would much prefer to think of ourselves as taking a position and choosing to speak out or remain silent on some well-reasoned, logical grounds.

Most folks are far more reactive, impulsive, situation-dependent and status-seeking in their responses than they imagine. It takes a controlled, laboratory situation to demonstrate these realities and even then, when told about such factors, most people believe it applies to others but not themselves -- "I would never do that; I'd stick up for what I thought!" The problem is that what a person thinks is quite changeable and most people are not aware of the inconsistencies in their shifting positions.

The way to avoid the pitfall of rationalization during your **Impact Review** is to resist trying to answer "why" and remain focused on "what". The first and most important step of an **Impact Review** is to carefully describe what happened: 1) the situation/context; 2) the persons and 3) the action.

Imagine that you are presenting your **Impact Review** to a colleague whose opinions and judgment you respect. This person respects and encourages you; you can tell this colleague anything. Imagine describing the situation thoroughly enough so that the colleague can see the scene in her/his mind's eye. Imagine describing the people sufficiently well that your colleague can *see* those people moving around in the situation you described. Finally, describe what happened with sufficient detail that your colleague not only understands the set-up and can see the people, but also understands what unfolded. You do not need to recall every word that was said, but you need to be able to describe what happened in the beginning, in the middle and how things ended.

As is true for **Impact Preview**, you may prefer to conduct your **Impact Review** with another person present. While you are still learning about these tools, you are more likely to move through all the steps and receive maximum benefit if you share your **Impact Review** with someone.

The second step of an **Impact Review** is to celebrate those aspects of the interaction that you approve of the way you directed and/or responded. Celebrate your having done an **Impact Preview** before the opening scene and celebrate what you did to make arrangements for the action to proceed one direction rather than another.

Since most of us are much better trained to confront the things we **failed** to do as well as the things we did and should **not** have, it will probably be very difficult to focus on the positive,  to-be-celebrated choices you made and actions you took without noting the negative choices and actions.  As long as you are making a list of those things to be celebrated, you can combine steps two and three: celebrate and confront.

Confronting those aspects of your performance which need to improve does not mean beating up on yourself. It is personally destructive to point out weaknesses in your performance and focus on how you fell short unless you move on to the fourth and final step of an **Impact Review** coaching yourself on how you could do it better next time.

Confronting weaknesses in your performance without coaching for improvement is guilt-inducing and shame-producing. That is neither fair nor effective. Confronting weakness in your performance, acknowledging it and coaching  yourself to improve provides the highest level of professionalism -- self evaluation and self regulation.

Imagine how you would coach a twelve year old neighbor kid on some set of skills you possess and the youngster is eager to learn. Imagine the youngster to be sincere, hard working, willing to try, committed to mastering whatever you are coaching, and therefore willing to practice. You know you would be far more encouraging than you would be harshly critical. You would not point out flaws and shortcomings and expect the youngster to identify the strengths and celebrate them on her/his own.

Be as gentle, as encouraging, as honest, as demanding, as specific, as thorough coaching yourself as you would be coaching the twelve year old neighbor kid. Once again, conducting an **Impact Review** in the presence of a *trusted other* increases the chances you will become as good a coach to yourself as you would be to the neighbor kid.

# NEM2 MasterStrategy®: Impact Now

The following brief description of **Impact Now** is offered for the purpose of having a sense of completion regarding applications of the **NEM2 MasterSkills®**. As we noted earlier, a real time application of the **NEM2 MasterSkills®** -- **Impact Now** -- is very much more difficult than **Impact Preview** or **Impact Review**. It is beyond the scope of this book to describe **Impact Now** with the same precision with which we have specified both **Impact Preview** and **Impact Review**.

To be able to observe and consciously make choices about your performance while in the midst of that performance requires the preparation of a professional jazz musician or improvisational actor. We believe that can be an appropriate expectation for anyone in a position of leadership who wants to be an excellent leader. However, before you could even entertain the possibility of taking action with **Impact Now**, you would have to have the three **NEM2 MasterSkills**® totally at your disposal -- available, regardless of the content, process or personnel with whom you are interacting.

Your co-workers will be very generous with you for any *genuine* effort -- however stumbling or awkward -- you make to listen to them with the **NEM2 MasterSkill**® *paraphrasing*. Your co-workers will also be very appreciative of any effort you make to clarify your purposes -- even if you forget and your **purpose stating** occurs in the middle of the interaction it should have preceded. You are very safe using both **Impact Preview** and **Impact Review** in the beginning or your pursuit of the **NEM2 MasterSkills**®. However, the intensity and performance demands of **Impact Now** should only be taken on, after you have had experience with the **NEM2 MasterSkills**® becoming **just the way you think and talk**.

Imagine a TV studio with three screens revealing what each of three cameras has in focus. Only one image is broadcast at any one time. It is the director's responsibility to decide moment-by-moment which image to broadcast. The three screens inside the control room and the three miniature screens on each camera that let the director and the camera operators know what each camera has in view are, of course, all called **monitors.**

The earliest experience most of us have with the concept of **monitoring** is in elementary schools. *Hall monitors, library monitors, lunch monitors, crosswalk monitors* usually are older students designated to help regulate the movement of people through the system's channels.

Imagine an intensive care unit in a nearby hospital. Most of you have seen either the real situation or a television version of an intensive care unit and are familiar with the electronic sounds corresponding to heart beats, the dots and lines on oscilloscopes corresponding to respiratory and brain functioning. All of these auditory and visual representations of a person's vital functions are ***monitors.***

***Monitoring*** in both of these contexts means regulating, helping stay in line, keeping things from going out of bounds, scanning and focusing in order to make the best decision. In each instance, in order to ***monitor*** effectively, a person needs:

1 an accurate, reliable picture of what is happening moment-by-moment

2 a clear understanding of the purpose desired and the range of tolerance associated with that ideal outcome

3 the power and ability to make decisions based on the incoming information in view of the purpose

***Impact Now*** is a self-monitoring process. The three **NEM2 MasterSkills®** -- ***paraphrasing, performance imaging and purpose stating*** -- are used in combination to regulate yourself while communication at work is in progress. Self monitoring requires that:

1  you observe yourself scanning and focusing in order to achieve a reliable, accurate picture of how things are impacting you and what impact you are having moment-by-moment

2  you consciously have in mind and can articulate behaviorally what your purposes and goals are

3  you have the skills and willingness to increase or decrease the intensity, frequency and/or timing of how you are moving and sounding according to the purposes you are trying to achieve.

For most of us, steering a car -- not driving the vehicle, but steering it -- is, in large part, an automatic, no-think process. There is very little conscious awareness of the dozens and dozens of choices that are involved in ordinary steering. We make these regulatory choices to *speed up, slow down, turn right, sharper left,* etc. without experiencing having made choices.

**Too often our self-monitoring of communication at work is more like *steering* than it is *driving* -- we make regulatory choices without having experienced ourselves as choosing.** *Impact Now* requires a vigilant, highly intentioned use of the **NEM2 MasterSkills®** to engage others in constructive communication at work.

Scanning and focusing in order to drive safely and within the speed limit can be very frustrating -- however, the consequences of failing to do so can be fatal!  Monitoring yourself interpersonally is very similar to monitoring your driving. Whether you need to slow down or speed up or refocus will depend upon your style, your purpose and the immediate situation. Ignoring the interpersonal impact you have at work can also be fatal.

# Chapter 6

## Continuous improvement in communication at work

***Continuous improvement*** is natural for humans. As we stated earlier (Chapter 3):

> Humans *do not inherit* very many skills, but humans do inherit the equipment to learn. Humans are born with very little information and ability, but humans are *hard-wired to acquire* an enormous range and amount of understanding and skill throughout their lives. . . . It is very **natural** for people to learn.

***Communication at work*** is also natural for humans. Howard Gardner, 1991, in the **Unschooled Mind**, comments on the extent to which:

> " . . . the human organism is pretuned to come to know the world of other persons. Beginning with the inclination of the newborn to focus on face-like configurations and the tendency of the two month old to smile when encountering another human being, infants emerge as incipient social psychologists, fascinated by other members of their species, no less than as fledgling physical scientists interested in the world on nonliving objects." (p. 50)

**Continuous improvement in communication at work** is completely natural for humans.

Humans are naturally active, social creatures -- we arrange to live, work and play in groups. What has become increasingly unhealthy for humans -- because they are so unnatural -- are the school, the workplace, and, sadly, the family. These institutions have, in fact, been very toxic for many, many people in the last one hundred years.

There are some signs of renewal in each of these institutions that, hopefully, will make it easier for the people comprising them to survive and flourish. The workplace was the first to recognize that the way we had structured work activity and the way people were asked to perform was suitable for machines, but not for living organisms. The workplace has led the way in making changes that are good for people. Warren Bennis, who has been a major voice for change in organizations for the last thirty years, wrote in the introduction to **Beyond Bureaucracy**, 1993, the reissued edition of his 1966 classic, **Changing Organizations**

> The autocratic man (and he was always a man) whose organization was his lengthened shadow is dead. The leaders of yesteryear were preoccupied with three objectives: control, order, and predictability. The post-bureaucratic organization requires a new kind of leader, one who can inspire and empower, who is maestro, not master; a coach, not a commander. . . .Tomorrow's organizations will be federations, networks, clusters, cross-functional teams, temporary systems, ad hoc task forces, lattices, modules, matrices, almost anything but pyramids.

In a perfect world, schools and homes would guarantee that everyone entering the work force would have the interpersonal core competencies required of a post-bu-reaucratic worker. However, following a discussion of *why the rich are getting richer and the poor, poorer,* Reich, 1991, makes it clear that training in interpersonal core competencies is not available to most school age children nor to most displaced and discouraged workers.

Unfortunately, for the foreseeable future, most people will be required to produce their own curriculum and self-evaluation system to learn the skills necessary -- espe-cially at an entry-level -- for communication at work. Hopefully, organizations will make a significant contribu-tion toward such training. That seems likely when you read declarations such as that of Richard Beckhard and Wendy Pritchard, 1992, identifying the key behavioral traits of thriving organizations redesigning themselves to confront an increasingly uncertain future:

- A superior ability to sense signals in the environment

- A strong sense of purpose

- The ability to manage toward visions

- Widely shared knowledge of where the organization is going

- An open culture with open communications

- A commitment to being a learning organization, with policies and practices that support this stance

- Valuing data and using it for planning both results and improvement

- High respect for individual contributions

- High respect for team and group efforts

- Explicit -- and continuing -- recognition of innovative and creative ideas and actions

- High tolerance for different styles

- High tolerance for uncertainty

- Structures that are driven by tasks

- High correlation between corporate or group visions and unit goals and strategies

- Good alignment between business goals and plans and the organization's capacity to perform

- The ability to successfully resolve the tension between high performance and continual performance

In view of this description of the *thriving organization of the future*, clearly, anyone in the workplace at any level, would be very well-served by the **NEM2 MasterSkills®**. In a very helpful futuristic view of how organizations must confront the increasing and inevitable tension between order and chaos entitled, ***Managing the Unknowable***, 1993, Stacey recommends that continuous learning programs similar to that described by Peter Senge, 1990, be built into organizations that hope to manage their unknowable futures. Interpersonal communication core competencies are a necessary part of *improving group learning skills*, recommended by Stacey.

You are most fortunate if you have access to a home or a school or a workplace that supports your continuous learning of core competencies for communication at work. However, if you must rely on yourself for learning these skills, we offer the following set of **Next Steps.**

# Next Steps . . .

As you know, we make the following claim:

> **Becoming competent using the three NEM2 MasterSkills® enables you to cope effectively with any and all interpersonal situations you confront in the workplace.**

**Learning Transfer Team Sessions** provide a way for the **NEM2 MasterSkills®** to be thoroughly learned and to be routinely put into practice.  Everyone agrees that:

- people learn more and better when they are teaching than when they are the passive recipients of others' teaching.

- people learn more and better when they are actively applying their learning to their own situations than when they merely think about the ways new insights might apply.

- people are more likely to follow through with applications and practice if they are accountable to their peers for doing so.

- people learn more and better when working on real issues with real colleagues, if that group of colleagues is safe -- that is, the group is small and its members are committed and constructive.

- practicing communication skill building takes time -- it cannot be accomplished overnight.

- coaching from a master teacher is most helpful, but self coaching with peer feedback and peer support are, also very powerful reinforcers.

We know that if people are truly intent on learning the **NEM2 MasterSkills**® they will commit themselves to becoming part of learning transfer teams to carry out the following exercises designed to facilitate practicing *paraphrasing, purpose stating* and *performance imaging*. We know that the **NEM2 MasterSkills**® cannot be learned and refined solely in a workshop training experience. Only by practice and practice-with-coaching beyond the training workshop can they be fully developed.

The following exercises have been designed to assist learning transfer teams practice and refine the **NEM2 MasterSkills**®. We know from our training experiences that those learning transfer teams who develop written contracts and make personal commitments to one another are more likely to have positive learning experiences and begin using the **NEM2 MasterSkills**® routinely in their daily work. We encourage you to develop a written contract with members of a learning transfer team.

## Transfer Team Guidelines

## The Contract

**MATERIALS:**     Each transfer team member has a blank CONTRACT form on which to draw up the team's agreements about your learning transfer sessions.

**PURPOSE:**     To increase the likelihood that learning transfer team members will sustain a constructive, collaborative process during their transfer sessions and will assist one another with continuous learning.

**PROCESSES:**  Examine the following list of concerns and issues about which people have expectations and can make clear agreements:

- confidentiality
- control
- cooperation
- criticism
- personal disclosures
- encouragement
- feedback

- honesty/frankness
- leadership
- outside assistance
- participation
- agreement departures
- time/punctuality
- vulnerability

Imagine what you might write if it were up to you to draft a set of guidelines or ground rules for your team. Try to clarify, in your own mind, what your preferences and your expectations are for the transfer team.

Discuss your preferences; identify easily agreed upon guidelines. Clarify the areas of greater disagreement. Come to some agreements about the disputed areas.

Select a Convenor for the first session; each session will need to close with selecting the Convenor for the next session. It is the Convenor's responsibility to see that team members are reminded about the meeting time and place and to alert team members to the amount of preparation which must precede the session. The Convenor arranges for whatever equipment is required. Summarize your agreements on the Contract Form and see that each person recieves a copy.

## "If I had it to do over . . . . "

Being able to review past performances allows people to see where they fell short and be able to think about better ways to manage themselves in future similar circumstances. Everyone experiences situations in the workplace that s/he would handle differently . . . if s/he had another opportunity. **"If I had it to do over . . ."** is a vehicle that encourages a person to learn from mistakes and/or disappointments. You will recognize this as an *Impact Review*.

**Before the transfer team meeting**, members should use *performance imaging* to identify a recent incident that probably could have been improved upon, if only they had listened more effectively -- they did not use *paraphrasing* as well as they could have -- or if only they had made their purposes clear -- they did not use *purpose stating*. These are "**If I had it to do over . . .** " episodes. Members should come prepared to talk about at least one.

**During the transfer team meeting**, members should tell their stories about "**If I had it to do over. . .**" incidents. No one is designated the *Facilitator* to paraphrase and purpose state; hopefully, team members will share the *purpose stating/paraphrasing* responsibility.

If a video camera is available to use, members should sit closely enough so that all of them are on camera; video tape the interaction. Observe any 5 minute section of the video and give feedback regarding *paraphrasing* and *purpose stating* in contrast to ignoring and/or questioning one another.

# Step Up to Strength

When asked to describe a workplace situation in which his/her performance was poor, the average person does not have any trouble remembering more than one episode. Additionally, s/he is not unwilling to discuss the situations. It is common place in many cultures for people to be quite willing and able to talk about their shortcomings, their weaknesses and their failings.

By contrast, when asked to describe competencies, personal strengths, ways they are proud of how they handled work situations -- most people become quite self-conscious and are unable to speak easily. There are many *lessons* learned in childhood which teach people to be modest, to be self-effacing, to let others do the bragging for us, to avoid sounding boastful in any situation -- to not think of ourselves more highly than we ought to think.

Becoming more matter-of-fact, objective and able to discuss strengths and vulnerabilities, victories and defeats, successes and failures -- both one's own and others' -- make collaboration more productive.

**Before the transfer team meeting**, members should identify three recent situations they handled very well. Members should use **performance imaging** to have these incidents clearly pictured so that they can recount the ways in which they believed they did an excellent job managing themselves.

Do an **Impact Preview** of how you expect to react to discussing your own positive performance with your co-workers.

**During the transfer team meeting,** members should take turns recounting the incidents in which they did an excellent job managing themselves. No one is designated *Facilitator* to **paraphrase** and **purpose state**; hopefully, team members will share the **paraphrasing/purpose stating** responsibility.

## Performance History

You are invited to examine the assumptions you make about becoming a more skillful interpersonal performer -- someone who is trying to improve people skills. You are asked to examine where some of your ideas about **performance**, in general, came from. Hopefully, you all may learn more about the development of your beliefs and attitudes towards **performance** which will make working on improving your interpersonal performances easier.

**Before the transfer team meeting**, use **performance imaging** to answer the following questions in preparation for the discussion:

- How was **performing** viewed by your family or peer group when you were growing up?

- What experiences **performing** did you have with music, dance, acting, reciting, speaking, reading, athletics?

- What was modeled by other family or peer group members?

- How did people teach you to distinguish between *performing* and *showing off*?

- How seriously were you regarded as a **performer**?

**At the meeting**, one member of the transfer team will offer to be the first person to be interviewed, the Presenter, and one to be the Facilitator and another to serve as Evaluator of the Facilitator's performance. The purposes of the Performance History interview are for the Facilitator to practice *paraphrasing* and *purpose stating* about topics that are likely to be personally meaningful to the Presenter and for the Evaluator to practice giving constructive feedback.

If a video camera is available, members should sit so that the Facilitator and the Presenter are on camera; video tape the interaction. Observe any 3-5 minute section of the video and have the Evaluator give feedback regarding the Facilitator's use of *paraphrasing and purpose stating* to communicate understanding of the Presenter's discussion.

When s/he has provided feedback, the other members of the transfer team can offer their feedback to the Facilitator.

# Put yourself in an unfamiliar setting

People, in general, stop focusing on familiar, repeating stimuli, e.g., clocks ticking, air conditioning hum, etc. A person's workplace is usually such a familiar setting. Workers often become so accustomed to these settings that they begin to function on *automatic pilot* -- an altered state of consciousness. The safety risks are apparent. But in addition, workers cease being aware of their impact on others, as well as others' impact on them.

In settings that are very different from those in which they spend most of their time, people pay closer attention to what they are doing, how they are feeling, what others are doing, how others appear to be reacting to them, etc. This alertness, focus, sensitivity is very valuable -- if the individual is able to regulate it -- if it does not control a person's thoughts, feelings and actions.

**Before the meeting,** each team member should select a setting with which s/he is completely unfamiliar. It could be a work setting or a social setting. For sure, it should be a safe setting. The team member should go alone to that setting and spend about an hour -- being open to any interpersonal interaction that might occur. S/he should attend to her/his thoughts, feelings and behaviors as the time passes and be prepared to talk about them at the transfer team meeting.

**At the meeting**, one member of the learning transfer team will offer to be the first person to be interviewed, i.e., the Presenter and one to be the Facilitator and another to serve as Evaluator of the Facilitator's performance. The purposes are for the Facilitator to use **paraphrasing** and

***purpose stating*** to understand information which is likely to be emotionally charged for the Presenter and for the Evaluator to practice giving constructive feedback.

If a video camera is available, members should sit so that the Facilitator and the Presenter are on camera; video tape the interaction. Observe any 3-5 minute section of the video and have the Evaluator give feedback regarding the Facilitator's use of ***paraphrasing and purpose stating*** to communicate understanding of the Presenter's story.

When s/he has provided feedback, the other members of the transfer team can offer their feedback to the Facilitator.

There, of course, is no end to continuous learning for communication at work. We could go on and on suggesting exercises and drills. If you have reached this point and followed through on the suggestions we have made, you can probably design whatever further polishing and fine-tuning you would need. However, **NEM2** has developed additional training games and exercises for each of the three **NEM2 MasterSkills**® and the **NEM2 MasterStrategies**®.

Contact Friendly Press if you wish to learn more about available materials.

# Communication at Work

# Sources

G. Bateson, *Mind and Nature*
Dutton, New York, 1979

R. Beckhard & W. Pritchard, *Changing the Essence*
Jossey-Bass, San Francisco, 1992

W. Bennis, *Why Leaders Can't Lead*
Jossey-Bass, San Francisco, 1989

W. Bennis, *Beyond Bureaucracy*
Jossey-Bass, San Francisco, 1993

H. Benson, *The Relaxation Response*
Morrow, New York, 1975

K. Blanchard & S. Johnson, *The One Minute Manager*
Berkley Books, New York, 1981

P. Block, *The Empowered Manager*
Jossey-Bass, San Francisco, 1987

J. Bowles & J. Hammond, **Beyond Quality**
Putnam, New York, 1991

J. P. Carse, *Finite and Infinite Games*
The Free Press, New York, 1986

P. B. Crosby, *Completeness*
Dutton, New York, 1992

P. B. Crosby, *Quality Without Tears*
McGraw, New York, 1985

# Sources

M. Davis et al, **The Relaxation and Stress Reduction Workbook,** New Harbinger, Oakland, 1988

S. M. Davis, **Future Perfect**
Addison-Wesley, Reading, 1987

E. de Bono, **de Bono's Thinking Course**
Facts on File, New York, 1982

M. DePree, **Leadership is an Art**
Dell, New York, 1989

M. DePree, **Leadership Jazz**
Doubleday, New York, 1992

H. Gardner, **The Unschooled Mind**
Basic Books, New York, 1991

J. W. Gardner, **Self-Renewal**
Norton, New York, 1981

C. Garfield, **Peak Performers**
Morrow, New York, 1986

S. Gawain, **Creative Visualization**
Whatever, Berkeley, 1978

E. Gendlin, **Focusing**
Bantam, New York, 1958

S. K. Gilmore, *A Comprehensive Theory for Eclectic Intervention*, Int. J. Coun. 3: 185 - 210 (1980), Nijhoff, The Hague, Netherlands

# Sources

J. Gleick, **Chaos**
  Penguin, New York, 1987

K. R. Hamamond (ed.), **The Psychology of Egon Brunswik**
  Holt, New York, 1966

C. Handy, **The Age of Unreason**
  Arrow Books, London, 1989

W. Harman, **Global Mind Change**
  Knowledge Systems, Indianapolis, 1988

F. Heider, **The Psychology of Interpersonal Relations**
  Wiley, New York, 1958

R. Kanter, **Change Masters**
  Simon & Schuster, New York, 1983

R. Kanter, **When Giants Learn to Dance**
  Simon & Schuster, New York, 1989

J. E. Loehr & J. A. Migdow, **Take a Deep Breath**
  Villard, New York, 1986

S. Ostrander & L. Schroeder, **Superlearning**
  Dell, New York, 1979

R. T. Pascale, **Managing on the Edge**
  Simon & Schuster, New York, 1990

F. D. Peat, **The Philosopher's Stone**
  Bantam, New York, 1991

# Sources

T. Peters, *Thriving on Chaos*
Harper, New York, 1987

B. Piazza, *The Exact and Very Strange Truth*
Farrar, Straus & Co., New York, 1964

J. Renesch ( ed.), *New Traditions in Business*
Sterling & Stone, San Francisco, 1991

E. Ristad, *A Soprano on Her Head*
Real People, Moab, 1982

K. D. Ryan & D. K. Oestreich, *Driving Fear out of the
Workplace,* Jossey-Bass, San Francisco, 1991

M. Samuels & N. Samuels, *Seeing with the Mind's Eye*
Random, New York, 1975

P. M. Senge, *The Fifth Discipline*
Doubleday, New York, 1990

R. D. Stacey, *Managing the Unknowable*
Jossey-Bass, San Francisco, 1992

J. Syer & C. Connnolly, *Sporting Body Sporting Mind*
Cambridge Univ. Press, London, 1984

M. J. Wheatley, *Leadership and the New Science*
Berrett-Koehler, New York, 1992

# Communication at Work

# Communication at Work

# Index

# Index

# Index

# Index

# Communication at Work